MW00717551

Bruce SPRINGSTEEN

Glory Days – 50 Years of Dreaming

First Published by FHE Ltd

This is an independent publication, it is unofficial and unauthorised and as such has no connection with the artist or artists featured, their management or any other organisation connected in any way whatsoever with the artist or artists featured. This book and DVD set contains no musical performances or compositions by the artist or artists featured.

The views in this publication are those of the authors but they are general views and whilst every effort has been made to ensure the accuracy of information within this publication the publisher shall have no liability to any person or entity with respect to inaccuracy, loss and or damage caused directly or indirectly by the information contained within this book.

All rights reserved, No part of this work may be produced or utilised in any form or by any means, electronic or mechanical, including photocopying or by any information storage and retrieval system, without prior written permission of the publisher.

CAT NO: ENB0300

Photography courtesy Pictorial Press, Wikimedia Commons, Getty Images unless indicated otherwise.

Made in EU.

ISBN: 978-0-9930170-7-0

CONTENTS

Chapter One

Bruce Springsteen once said: *"I want it all."* People these days often forget that, baffled by an artist whose musical output can switch, seemingly effortlessly, from the gung-ho R&B swing of classic rock albums like 'Born To Run' or, still his biggest-seller, 'Born In The USA', to the heartrendingly stark acoustic outpourings of albums like 'Nebraska' and 'The Ghost Of Tom Joad' – or even more perplexing for some, the most recent collection of venerable folk and country covers, 'We Shall Overcome: The Seeger Session'.

It's a confusion that goes right back to his earliest days as a recording artist, when he was still seen as some sort of folksy troubadour in the tradition of Bob Dylan. For Springsteen himself, however, there has never been any difference between the outgoing crowd-pleaser of hits like 'Hungry Heart' and the introspective loner of 'Secret Garden'. As far as he was concerned, music was one of the few things in life that held no barriers. As he explained in a 1992 interview with New York Newsday: *"When I was young, I truly didn't think music had any limitations. I thought it could give you everything you wanted in life."*

For Robert Hilburn of the LA Times, Springsteen would come to define *"the struggle in life between disillusionment and dreams."* Adding: *"The important thing about Bruce isn't that he makes you believe in rock and roll or himself. He makes you believe in yourself."* While Dave Marsh of Rolling Stone suggested that Springsteen's best music was nothing less than *"a refutation of the idea that rock was anarchic rebellion. If anything, his shows were a masterwork of crowd control, an adventure in pure cooperation, a challenge to chaos."*

But, as usual, Springsteen put it best himself in his thank-you speech when 'Streets Of Philadelphia' won him the Oscar in 1994 for Best Original Song In A Movie: *"You do your best work and you hope that it pulls out the best in your audience and some piece of it spills over into the real world and into people's everyday lives. And it takes the edge off fear and allows us to recognise each other through our veil of differences. I always thought that was one of the things popular art was supposed to be about, along with the merchandising and all the other stuff."*

Destined to become the blue-collar rock hero whose best songs represented the common experiences of everyday American people, Bruce Springsteen was born to working-class Irish-Italian parents in the modest New Jersey town of Freehold, on the 23rd of September 1949. His Irish-descendent father, Douglas Springsteen, was an-ex army recruit who later worked in a plastics factory, as a bus driver and a prison guard. Bruce was the first of three children, and his Italian mother, Adele, worked hard to provide a home for them all. His early life was not without its inequities, however, and Springsteen would later recall the harsh nature of the Catholic school he attended as a child. One story, in particular, continued to haunt him into adulthood, when, as an eight-year-old, he got his Latin wrong and the nun who taught him stood him in the wastebasket because *"that's what you are worth"*. As a result, by his won admission, he loathed school and learned little other than what it was like to be the victim of intolerance and prejudice. When not in school, he liked hanging around on the beach and playing water sports. He was never a talkative boy, though, preferring to watch and listen, standing in the shadows taking it all in.

Little Bruce first started playing guitar at the age of nine after seeing Elvis Presley on TV. He got his first blasts of loud music from listening to the radio. *"It took over my whole life,"* he later explained. *"Everything from then on revolved around music."*

Springsteen attended his first gig at the age of 12 when his mother Adele whisked her son and her eldest daughter Ginny off for a day in Atlantic City, roughly 15 miles from Freehold. There, at Steel Pier, they saw Chubby Checker – 'Mr. Twist' – play a matinee, and they took in another show by singer Anita Bryant before heading homewards.

By the time he entered his teens, Springsteen had acquired a second-hand guitar that he paid for from odd jobs. His cousin Frankie, a guitar and accordion player, gave young Bruce some lessons, beginning with 'Greensleeves'. Not a belter exactly, but it was a start. Springsteen would belatedly return the favour by inviting Frankie onstage with him at major American venues.

Two things happened in September 1963. Bruce turned 14. And he started his freshman year at Freehold Regional High School, relieved to be free of the severely enforced discipline of the Catholic education he'd received at St Rose Of Lima. His interest in music had been growing, but when he saw The Beatles' legendary appearances on The Ed Sullivan Show over three consecutive weeks in February 1964 – kick-starting the 'British Invasion' of America – his excitement was almost uncontrollable. This truly was music by the young for the young.

Bruce Springsteen returned to his acoustic guitar with renewed determination, already dreaming of a shiny new electric model and an amp. He kept on watching Ed Sullivan, who delivered The Dave Clark Five, The Animals, The Rolling Stones and The Kinks to massive TV audiences. Springsteen was especially fired up by the roughneck blues and R&B drive of The Animals and the Stones, although he'd already watched in awe as an audacious, pouting Mick Jagger led the band through their debut American TV appearance on Hollywood Palace in June 1964 – an occasion which inspired the even younger Steven Van Zandt, watching in Middletown, NJ to pick up a guitar and play. Bruce also loved the sound of female vocal groups such as The Ronettes.

That year, Christmas came with everything he could have hoped for. His mother, a secretary, had taken out a loan of $60 to present him with a Kent electric guitar and amp.

Within six months, her son was playing that same guitar in his first band, taking his initial steps towards a future that would see him hailed across the world as The Boss.

However, it would be wrong to say that the path to superstardom ran especially smoothly in the Springsteen household, if Bruce himself is to believed.

As he would often explain to an audience in the mid-70s, just before launching into one of his favourite songs from his childhood, The Animals' 'It's My Life', "*I grew up in this small town about 20 miles inland. I remember it was in this dumpy, two-storey, two-family house, next door to this gas station. And my mom, she was a secretary and she worked downtown. And*

Chapter One

my father, he worked a lotta different places, worked in a rug mill for a while, and he was a guard down at the jail for a while. I can remember when he worked down there, he used to come back real pissed off, drunk, sit in the kitchen. At night, about nine o'clock, he used to shut off all the lights, every light in the house. And he'd sit in the kitchen with a six-pack and a cigarette. (When I got home) I'd stand there in that driveway, afraid to go in the house, and I could see the screen door, I could see the light of my pop's cigarette. I used to slick my hair back real tight so he couldn't tell how long it was gettin' and try to sneak through the kitchen. But the old man, he'd catch me every night and he'd drag me back into that kitchen. He'd make me sit down at that table in the dark, and he would sit there tellin' me. And I can remember just sittin' there in the dark, him tellin' me... tellin' me, tellin' me, tellin' me.

Pretty soon he'd ask me what I thought I was doin' with myself, and we'd always end up screamin' at each other. My mother, she'd always end up runnin' in from the front room cryin' and tryin' to pull him off me, try to keep us from fightin' with each other. And I'd always, I'd always end up runnin' out the back door, pullin' away from him, runnin' down the driveway, screamin' at him, tellin' him, tellin' him, tellin' him how it was my life and I was gonna do what I wanted to do."

In those early days, US radio was the home not just of Elvis Presley and Chuck Berry, it was a direct route to another world, aimed at the very soul of a sprawling teenage America, from the rural heartlands to the inner city and boardwalks of Bruce's childhood. If it got on the radio that meant it usually got into the juke-boxes of the numerous diners, soda fountains and truck stops that littered the nation, too. This was where the teenage Bruce first got the strange idea that rock'n'roll could matter, as well as entertain; could make you think as well as dance. It was a lesson he absorbed quickly; one he never forgot.

"What I heard in The Drifters, in all that great radio music, was the promise of something else. Not a politician's promise... I mean the promise of possibilities... that the search and the struggle matter, that they affirm your life." As he saw it, *"That was the original spirit of rock'n'roll."*

But if rock'n'roll spelled 'freedom' in the more general sense to countless millions of teenagers in the cultural melting pot of 1960s' America, it took on quite literal properties to Springsteen, whose parents moved from Freehold down to San Francisco when he was 17. By then, he had already auditioned for a guitarist's job in his first band, The Castiles, and was promptly snapped up by the band's manager, the wonderfully named Tex Vinyard, and the band. The Castiles' frontman was George Theiss, a classmate and admirer of Bruce's sister Ginny, and the band consisted of Theiss, Bart Haynes (drums), Frank Marziotti (bass) and Paul Popkin (harmony vocals). Springsteen made his live debut with them just

a few weeks later, so he decided to stay behind in Jersey, moving into a scruffy one-room apartment above a drug store in nearby Long Branch. It was around this time that he also began appearing occasionally as a solo act at the Café Wha? in Greenwich Village: the same venue in which a similarly young Dylan had first become recognised. Commuting between Asbury Park and downtown New York, *"I was always popular in my little area, and I needed this gig badly. I didn't have anything else. I wanted to be as big as you could make it... the Beatles, the Rolling Stones."*

The Castiles treated their first couple of gigs, around the Freehold area, as warm-ups, playing for free. Springsteen's first paid show with The Castiles, receiving the grand sum of $35, was at the Woodhaven Swim Club. Memorably, the group finished their set with a roughed-up version of 'In The Mood', a big-band song made popular by American bandleader Glenn Miller. Most of the songs in their live set were covers, including British Invasion favourites: The Stones' 'Satisfaction' and 'The Last Time', The Beatles' 'Till There Was You', The Zombies' 'For Your Love' and The Kinks' 'Tired Of Waiting For You'.

Depending on their audience – for The Castiles were as likely to turn out for a wedding reception or a supermarket opening as a regular rock gig – they might slip in an old standard or two, 'Summertime' maybe, or 'Stranger On The Shore'.

It was in The Castiles that Springsteen first performed an original song in public. Legend has it that two fans at a gig in Port Monmouth's Teen Club presented him with some lines of lyrics, which he then worked up into a soul song called 'Sidewalk'. This became a highlight of the set, with audiences often demanding to hear it several times a night – a huge vote of confidence in Springsteen as a writer and performer.

Towards the end of 1965, Bart Haynes abruptly walked out on the band. Within two years he would be dead, killed in action as a US Marine in the Vietnam War. The Castiles replaced him with drummer Vinny Manniello. Then Frank Marziotti left, to be succeeded by bassist Curt Fluhr.

The Castiles carried on playing around New Jersey throughout 1966 and beyond, anywhere they could get a gig. Their itinerary took in clubs, psychiatric hospitals, high schools (including Bruce's), teen dances, drive-in movies, charity benefits, trailer parks, roller dromes, birthday parties, private functions and battle-of-the-bands competitions, which they never won. On one occasion, they lost out to The Shadows – a group that included Steven Van Zandt.

Springsteen was taking on board a whole host of new musical influences. He still adored the big British pop, rock and blues bands, finally getting to see a couple of them in the flesh when The Who supported Herman's Hermits (!) at the Asbury Park Convention Hall on August

Chapter One

Bruce Springsteen *Glory Days – 50 Years of Dreaming*

the 12th 1967. He had also taken an interest in folk artists and singer-songwriters including Bob Dylan, Judy Collins and Donovan, and in the psychedelic rock sounds arising from the Summer Of Love. The Castiles' set reflected these broadening tastes and with Springsteen now delivering the bulk of the lead vocals and the band having added an organist, Bob Alfano, their covers became more ambitious. Their autumn 1967 sets included Jimi Hendrix's 'Purple Haze' and 'Hey Joe', Moby Grape's 'Omaha', Donovan's 'Catch The Wind' and Leonard Cohen's 'Suzanne', alongside selections from The Beatles, The Yardbirds, The Who, The Kinks and The Bee Gees. Also aired at this time was an original song called 'Look Into My Window', co-written by Springsteen and George Theiss.

And the crowds still called for 'Sidewalk'.

As their repertoire expanded, so The Castiles began travelling beyond their own Garden State.

Too poor to pay for his own entertainment, when he wasn't working he trod the boardwalks by the beach in Asbury. Outgoing and talkative onstage, off it he could be almost unbearably shy, mumbling his conversation and shuffling around in old clothes he looked like he'd slept in. "Jersey," he later moaned in a Sound article in March 1974, was "a dumpy joint. I mean it's OK, it's home, but... I guess it just took a long time for someone to think of something to write about it."

It hardly seems credible now, but the teenage Springsteen's career nearly took a very different course when, in 1968, he received his draft papers into the US army. With the US then involved in the Vietnam war, like all new conscripts young Bruce knew his chance of escaping the conflict without being maimed or killed was 50-50 at best, and years later he confessed that he and his buddies went out and got good and drunk the night before they were due to be inducted. When, though, the teenager flunked his medical, in large part due to injuries he had sustained in a motorcycle accident some time before, he returned home that day fearing the reaction such news would be greeted with by his ex-army father. Instead of disparaging the boy, however, Springsteen Senior merely nodded and said, "That's good, son." The subject was never mentioned again, although it was something he would return to in his own mind a great deal over the years (not least after the news that Bart Haynes had been killed in the conflict).

Instead, Springsteen spent most of his youth hanging out at a local 'teen club' named the Upstage – an avowedly alcohol and drug-free environment situated down by the Jersey shoreline which, nevertheless, stayed open till five every morning and where any passing kid with enough nerve could get up and play. This was where Springsteen and his friends first played as The Castiles, quickly followed by similarly short-lived but evermore adept outfits like Earth, Child, Steel Mill, Dr Zoom & The Sonic Boom and, finally in his early 20s, the more prosaically named Bruce Springsteen Band, a sprawling ten-piece back-up group (three members of which would later form part of his next legendary backing outfit, the E Street Band).

E Street was actually where the mother of the band's original keyboard player, David Sancious, lived, in the Jersey neighbourhood of Belmar.

It wasn't until 1975 that the best-known line-up of the E Street Band came together, though, when Springsteen was already well-known enough to attract Broadway show veterans like Weinberg and Bittan, who both responded to an ad in the Village Voice, rather than simply gravitating towards the line-up from the local Shore club scene. First, though, Springsteen would need to secure a record deal.

Ironically, this only transpired once Springsteen had all but abandoned the idea of getting his own band off the ground. Years of opening for every band that came through town, from Black Oak Arkansas and Brownsville Station to Sha Na Na and Black Sabbath, had left him weary and disillusioned. "When we first started playing", he commented years later, "I'd go to every show expecting nobody to come, and I'd go onstage expecting nobody to give me anything for free. And that's the way you have to play. If you don't play like that, pack your guitar up, throw it in the trashcan and go home... The night I stop thinking that way, that's the night I won't do it anymore."

At which point, he later told NME, he fell out of love with the idea of being in a band and "just started writing lyrics, which I had never done before. I would just get a good riff, and as long as it wasn't too obtuse I'd sing it... Last winter ('72) I wrote like a madman... Had no money, nowhere to go, nothing to do... It was cold and I wrote a lot... I got to feeling guilty if I didn't."

It was this batch of songs that would lead directly to his signing as a solo artist to Columbia Records, in New York, in May 1972. At first, he was seen by the label's A&R chief, John Hammond, as a potential successor to Bob Dylan – who he had also signed to the label some ten years before. In retrospect, it's easy to see why Hammond thought this way. Curly-haired and bearded, the 23-year-old Springsteen definitely had something of the wordy young Dylan about him, especially in early original songs like 'Blinded By The Light' and 'It's Hard To Be A Saint In The City'.

As he later told Zigzag magazine, playing the bars and clubs of his youth, "you had to communicate on the most basic level... but when I talked to the record companies there was just me by myself with a guitar, and from that many false impressions were drawn".

At the time, Dylan was a conspicuous influence on a generation of new young songwriters, many of whom had already suffered from the comparison: talented word-and-tunesmiths like John Prine and Loudon

Wainwright III, both of whom would struggle under Dylan's shadow throughout their early careers, the 'new Dylan' tag acting almost like a curse. Bruce, however, was not so easily subsumed.

Nevertheless, the comparisons were perhaps even more obvious in early Springsteen songs. As his first manager, Mike Appel pointed out: *"Bruce is very garrulous".*

As Appel would later tell the NME in an October 1973 interview: *"When I first came across Bruce it was by accident. But when I heard him play, I heard this voice saying to me – superstar. I couldn't believe it. I'd never been that close to a superstar before."* He added: *"Randy Newman is great but he's not touched. Joni Mitchell is great but she's not touched. Bruce is touched... he's a genius!"*

It was Appel that had taken acetates of Springsteen's earliest songs to Hammond – a legendary figure at Columbia who had also signed such pre-Dylan luminaries to the label as Louis Armstrong, Bessie Smith, Billie Holiday, Tommy Dorsey, and Woody Herman, to name just a few. Hammond listened to the acetate while Mike and Bruce sat patiently in the corner. *"Do you want to get your guitar out,"* Hammond eventually asked, at which point Bruce broke into a spontaneous version of 'It's Hard To Be A Saint In The City'. *"I couldn't believe it. I just couldn't believe it",* Hammond later recalled. Intrigued by the rough recordings and charmed by the soft-spoken young protégé, Hammond had gone straight to Columbia president Clive Davis, who famously rubber-stamped the whole deal after listening to just one track.

It was still live onstage, however, that the young Springsteen made the greatest impact. At a time when most singer-songwriters tended towards a more low-profile performance, either sitting alone with their guitars and standing still in the spotlight, Bruce had spent almost all his initial record advance on putting a new band of friends together, hitting the road even before his first album was released; it was entitled 'Greetings From Asbury Park NJ' and released in March 1973. Recorded at 914 Sound Studios, in Blauvelt, New York, and co-produced by Mike Appel and Jim Cretecos, the backing musicians featured on it were drummer Vini 'Mad Dog' Lopez, saxophonist Clarence Clemons, bassist Gary Tallent and keyboard player David Sancious – all of whom would go on to form the backbone of the next Springsteen live band – plus session-men Harold Wheeler and Richard Davis. The sleeve was based on a mock picture-postcard of Asbury Park, somewhat worn around the edges: a suitable visual metaphor for the forlorn picture of boardwalk life the music evoked.

Regarded, not unfairly, as overly self-conscious, with the lyrics tending to overshadow the music to an almost unprecedented degree, even for a would-be 'new Dylan', Columbia chose to promote the album by releasing as a first single one of the most lyrically verbose songs on an album almost choking with words: 'Blinded By The Light'. Needless to say, it was not a hit and despite mostly positive, if somewhat lukewarm reviews in the US, the album did not sell well either (although Britain's Manfred Mann would manage to take their more musically florid version of 'Blinded By The Light' to Number 1 in the US charts when it was released as a single in 1976). Nevertheless, there were several golden nuggets in amongst the slush-pile of semi-autobiographical journal entries. Not least one of the tracks that had helped secure him his deal: the epochal 'It's Hard To Be A Saint In The City', which closed the album and pointed the way in which later, more musically adept Springsteen albums would evolve.

Later covered by David Bowie for inclusion on his 1975 'Young Americans' album, though it never made the final cut, Bowie, then enjoying the first flush of his huge worldwide success, let it be known how much he loved the album (actually recording a second track from it, 'Growin' Up', though that also failed to make the final 'Young Americans' track-listing), and suddenly, despite its lack of sales, 'Greetings...' became one of the most-discussed albums by a new artist in 1973.

Other first-album tracks like 'Spirit In The Night' and 'Lost In The Flood' are also worth a special mention as they would go on to become live favourites for years; the former a funky R&B number you could actually dance to (unlike most of the other relentlessly edgy tracks on the album); the latter an apocalyptic soul-barer that prefigured some of Springsteen's later, more determinedly downbeat moments like 'The River'. While 'Does This Bus Stop At 82nd Street' sounded like it could have been written for an earlier generation by a young, chain-smoking, Benzedrine-swallowing Jack Kerouac.

Despite the dense lyrical undergrowth of so much of the album, according to Springsteen much of it was actually written quickly with barely any second thoughts at all. Tracks like the "suicide ballad" 'For You' (which recounts the final minutes of a life) and 'The Angel' (a view of life's highway taken astride a purring motorcycle) were, he later claimed, written in under 15 minutes. *"I see these situations happening when I sing them, and I know the characters well – they're probably based on people I know... It's like if you're walking down the street, that's what you see, but a lot of the songs were written without any music at all."*

As he told Zigzag: *"That record reflects the mood I was in at that particular time... you know, the fact of having to come into the city from where I was living, and I didn't have a band, so it all contributed to that kind of down feel. But towards the end of the record, I started pulling out of it with songs like 'Spirit In The Night' which started to get into a whole different feel."*

For all its virtues and critical support, 'Greetings...' remains one of the least approachable of Springsteen's earliest albums; capturing the artist at his most determinedly demented; so desperate to be taken seriously he appears, at times, to have forgotten what fun he used to have simply standing up there onstage singing. To his credit, it was a mistake he would be careful not to repeat on his next album. Before he started work on that, however, Springsteen and his band would complete over 200 gigs around the US, sometimes supporting bigger established acts like Chicago, most often playing one-nighters at clubs and bars along the East Coast. It was a punishing schedule that found Bruce and his boys getting by on a couple of bucks a day each, dining on hamburgers and beer. But it was also one that would prove to be the making of the band – now named the E Street Band – tightening them up and helping flesh-out songs like 'Spirit In The Night' and 'For You' that had sounded stilted on album, transforming them into sure-fire crowd-pleasers.

They went on the road to promote Greetings From Asbury Park, NJ at the end of October 1972, well before the album was released, taking with them as sound manager Albee Tellone, who had previously contributed sax and vocals to Friendly Enemies and Dr Zoom.

And although they did not have the funding to undertake a full-scale national tour, they got around many parts of the United States that they hadn't seen before, and they played so many gigs that their itinerary would merge seamlessly with the rash of dates set up to support the second album.

The never-ending roadshow opened with a third-on-the-bill support to freak-culture comedians Cheech & Chong at West Chester College, Pennsylvania, on October the 28th. It was not an auspicious beginning to the tour: the headlining duo's representatives flew into a tizzy, claiming not to have known that Springsteen was on the bill, and he was forced to cut short his set after only a few songs.

The next night, at the National Guard Armory at Long Branch, NJ, Springsteen perfected the stage routine he would prefer for the foreseeable future, appearing on his own at first to play a few songs before bringing on the band. By now, a real chemistry was developing between Springsteen and Clarence 'The Big Man' Clemons, and their bantering double act would become one of the band's biggest attractions.

They supported Crazy Horse in York, Pennsylvania, and Sha Na Na and Brownsville Station in Dayton and Columbus, Ohio, although they would usually headline their own shows when they performed in New Jersey and The Big Apple.

Yet nothing could hold a candle to the happenings of April the 28th 1973 when Springsteen lived a night that will stay with him forever.

Not only did the band open for Jerry Lee Lewis and Chuck Berry at the University of Maryland College Park, but they also formed the backing band for Berry, joined by their old Asbury Park friend Southside Johnny.

Springsteen had long been a fan of Berry, having worked his way back to the source after thrilling to The Rolling Stones' covers and Keith Richards' guitar licks. He knew the songs back to front and had played some of them onstage. He was aware that Berry was a lone wolf, using local bands to back him in almost every town he played. Bruce lobbied successfully for his band, and not a local one, to perform the back-up duties for his hero in Maryland – for free. What Bruce didn't realise was that Berry was not a man for rehearsal or consultation. He expected each night's musicians to lock into his set immediately and intuitively. Springsteen recalls the evening with much laughter in the Chuck Berry documentary, Hail!

'When we went down to Maryland, we drove in from some overnight gig, I forget where from (the Ohio festival) and we came out, we played about a half hour, which is generally the time you were allotted in those days if you were an opening act. We went over pretty good and then Jerry Lee Lewis came out and he did his set, standing on the piano, and... no Chuck Berry. No – he's not there. I forget what time he was supposed to go on, but it was getting very close... and there was no sign of him. The promoter was getting really nervous... About five minutes before the show was timed to start, the back door opens and he comes in by himself and he's got a guitar case and that was it. I guess he rolled up in his own car or something – there wasn't anybody with him. And he kinda walked by me and went straight to the office with the promoter. I guess the rumour was that he would get 11 grand and at the end of the night he'd give a grand back if the band was okay and if the equipment worked. I don't know if that's true, but that was what we heard.

So. Straight into the office, and then he walks out of the office and he comes into the band room. We says, "*Well, Chuck, what songs are we gonna do?*" He says, "*Well, we're gonna do some Chuck Berry songs*". That's all he said. So we go, "*Okay*". We get out onstage. The crowd's going insane – they can see him. He walks on, opens up the guitar case, tunes the guitar. The lights are up; the place is going nuts and we're going, "*What are we going to start with? Chuck?*" And he's kinda not paying attention to us, not hearing us."

The next thing Bruce heard was the sound of Berry launching into one of his time-honoured riffs.

"*And, like, we're in a state of total panic. We're trying to figure out – "What song are we playing? What key is it in?*" And Chuck plays in a lot of strange keys, like B flat, E flat, and our bass player is kind of the historian of the band so everybody runs to him and he has the right key. And so we pick up the key and we're doing pretty good, I think.

I forget what song it was, but we're playing away and the crowd's going nuts and Chuck runs back and says, *"Play for that money, boys!"* We forgot to tell him we weren't getting any money, we're doing this for free. Anyway, the night ended, there was a big brawl in front of the stage and the lights came on and I think his amp blew up. I guess we were doing 'Johnny B Goode' by now, just playing that rhythm, and he just walked off the stage, right to the side of the stage, packed his guitar in front of the entire auditorium, they're going crazy, and he waved and that was it. He walked out and walked back into his car and he was gone...

I doubt that he'd remember us, but it was just that kinda night that you know, when I'm 65, 70, I got my grandkids – *"Chuck Berry, yeah I met Chuck Berry... matter of fact, I backed Chuck Berry up one night." "You did?" "Yeah." It's a story I'm always gonna tell."*

Despite the constant touring and the vigorous crowd responses to the live Bruce Springsteen experience, Greetings From Asbury Park, NJ still wasn't seeing much action. It failed to chart in either America or the UK. Columbia's response was to send the band back into 914 Sound Studios in the summer of 1973 to record another album with Mike Appel and Jim Cretecos again at the helm – just four months after the release of Greetings.

The sessions took place in a piecemeal fashion, between gigs. Life was exhausting. There was no let-up in the sheer volume of bookings, the headlining appearances in clubs and colleges, and the support shows with major rock acts. Bruce Springsteen may have been signed to one of the biggest recording companies in the world, but neither he nor his band received any favours on the road. Everyone was broke. There were no hotels, no trains, no planes, no shiny tour buses. Bruce and the boys travelled together in a station wagon, sharing out the driving duties – although it must be said that Springsteen, a hair-raising driver, wasn't often chosen. Danny Federici was a willing volunteer, but he wasn't a lot better than Bruce, his sense of direction occasionally leading the entourage far from where they wanted to be, their equipment trundling along behind them, in a van. They would sometimes drive for hundreds of miles from one gig to the next, and it was a bonding lifestyle, one that consolidated their drive to succeed.

Springsteen recalled, *"None of us had even been on an airplane until we were on our way to a CBS convention in Los Angeles."* He was probably referring to a series of seven public concerts staged by CBS at the Ahmanson Theatre in LA under the banner of 'A Week To Remember', each night showcasing three company bands. Springsteen appeared on May 1st, opening for Doctor Hook and New Riders Of The Purple Sage.

It was an eventful summer. On May the 30th, the band began a 12-date support tour with Chicago in Fayetteville, North Carolina. It included two shows, on June the 14th and 15th, at New York's vast Madison Square Garden, where Chicago's fans took no interest in Springsteen and lacked the manners to watch his set politely, if at all. Springsteen vowed never to play such enormous venues again, and he was as good as his word for several years.

In other ways, the tour had been a disappointment. Unlike some of the more accommodating headliners they'd worked with, Chicago insisted that Springsteen must play only 45 minutes. The band, who had really started to flex their muscles live and were used to playing two-hour sets, complained that this didn't give them enough time to work up a decent head of steam. The Eagles' Don Henley was one person who probably wouldn't have sympathised too much: having watched Springsteen's performance at a music festival in Athens, Ohio, back in April, an impressed Henley predicted that he wouldn't be a supporting player for much longer.

A week after the Chicago shows had ended so unfortunately at Madison Square Garden, the band were back in the more familiar surroundings of New Jersey's clubland on June the 22nd with the first of three headline gigs at Fat City in Seaside Heights. And now there were six people onstage. David Sancious had finally agreed to join as a second keyboard player – or a third, counting Springsteen's own piano outings. Bruce had felt for some time that the band needed a plumper sound, and when he heard that David had returned to Asbury Park, he invited him again to join the line-up. With Sancious, a devoted jazz fan, on board, the group not only achieved a fuller sound but they were also able to explore more diverse textures, timings and arrangements.

Sancious joined the group after they'd completed most of the basic recordings for the seven tracks that would make up the second album – The Wild, The Innocent & The E Street Shuffle. The original five band members had worked quickly in the studio – they lacked the luxury of time and money, and they had already rounded out two of the songs in their live performances. 'Rosalita (Come Out Tonight)' was a rousing if irregular inclusion in the set; 'Wild Billy's Circus Story' was more familiar, even if fans knew it by the name of 'Circus Song'. To add to the confusion, its first title was 'Circus Town'.

Sancious, in a series of sporadic sessions stretching into the autumn of 1973, overdubbed his parts onto the existing tracks. It was also during this period that the extra musicians on the album recorded their contributions, namely Suki Lahav (backing vocals), Richard Blackwell (congas and percussion), and saxophonist turned soundman turned soundman-and-saxophonist, Albee Tellone.

There are some but not many people lucky enough to have seen the bands appearing together at Max's Kansas City twice every night between July the 18th and 23rd. Bruce Springsteen was the main attraction in the intimate New York hotspot. And his support act was Bob Marley and The Wailers, making their first inroads into the United States.

By this time, more of the new songs were turning up in the set. 'New York City Serenade' and the sensational ballad '4th Of July, Asbury Park (Sandy)' joined staples such as 'Thundercrack', Greetings favourites 'Spirit In The Night', 'It's Hard To Be A Saint In The City' and 'Does This Bus Stop At 82nd Street?', and covers of R&B classics including 'Route 66'. And wherever the band played, more and more people were becoming convinced that they were witnessing history in the making. Playing a return residency at Oliver's in Boston in August, Springsteen came as a revelation to Boston Globe reviewer Neal Vitale, who wrote: *The feeling was that of having seen a totally brilliant, unique, soon-to-be-a-giant artist in his early days before he becomes a star."*

In November, at a college gig in Hampden Sydney, Virginia, Springsteen gave 'The E Street Shuffle' its live debut, summoning Albee Tellone away from his sound duties for five minutes to come onstage and play some baritone sax. Tellone would continue to guest on this number at live gigs until the end of the year, when he left the party to form his own group.

'E Street' was a name that struck a chord with Springsteen shortly after David Sancious joined the band. Travelling back from a gig, they were dropping David off at his Jersey Shore home in Belmar in the early hours of the morning when Bruce spotted the name on a street sign. According to Sancious, Springsteen immediately began repeating 'E Street Band'. However, the first use of the E Street name came with 'The E Street Shuffle' (one of the last songs written and recorded for the new album). If Springsteen had indeed named the band at this point, then they kept it in the family for the time being.

The Greetings tour finally came to an end in October in Villanova, Philadelphia, where Springsteen played a co-headline show with Jackson Browne. The latter subsequently described it as *"a truly magical night".* One week later, the band jumped back into the station wagon to start promoting 'The Wild, The Innocent & The E Street Shuffle', which was set for US release in November (and in the UK, February 1974).

Bruce was also finding time to build in some of the new numbers he was now writing with the band very much in mind; warmer, less wooden-sounding material like 'Kitty's Back', which, built around a lengthy crescendo-building keyboard intro from David Sancious, had become one of the highlights of the set. With the newfound freedom and confidence his band was giving him, Springsteen suddenly sounded less like a poor

Bruce Springsteen *Glory Days - 50 Years of Dreaming*

man's Bob Dylan and more like a younger, more carefree Van Morrison.

This was the backdrop that would lead to the recording of what would be the first really convincing Bruce Springsteen album, the joyously titled 'The Wild, The Innocent And The E Street Shuffle'.

Recorded at the tail end of 1973 and released in February 1974, the second Springsteen album was the first to really capture what quickly became known as the signature E Street sound. Indeed, in its varied and often esoteric choice of instrumentation, it remains one of the most adventurous musical statements either Springsteen or the E Street Band would ever make: Bruce on acoustic as well as electric guitar, Danny Federici on accordion as well as keyboards, Garry Tallent on tuba as well as bass.

It was also a record practically overflowing with syncopated beats, jazz riffs, soul horns, and an array of typically colourful street 'characters'. As Springsteen later explained, he had been searching for a sound that *"rocks a little differently – more in the rhythm and blues vein"*. The fact that he achieved that goal on his second album was almost entirely down to the band he had assembled, a fact partly acknowledged in the album's elongated title. Most prominent was the influence of Clarence Clemons, Garry Tallent and David Sancious, who between them had a wealth of experience playing soul, jazz and R&B on the black West Side of Jersey.

The songs seem less stridently personal, too, and more story-based tracks – like the wheezing 'Wild Billy's Circus Story', the jazzy 'Incident On 57th Street' (which he was still introducing onstage as 'Spanish Johnny') and the dreamy 'New York City Serenade', or the demi-title track, 'E Street Shuffle' (featuring gritty Stax-styled guitar), even his first full-blown love song, '4th Of July. Asbury Park (Sandy)' – lyrically, all found the chief protagonist looking out instead of staring inwards. Best of all there was for the first time of a real sense of fun to be found in the record's grooves, as evidenced on the album's most effervescent moment, the raucous 'Rosalita'. As later seen on the famous Old Grey Whistle Test TV clip, 'Rosalita' was not only the highlight of the Springsteen live show, it was Bruce's own new favourite; the song that best captured the bristling energy he and his new band were able to summon forth when the spirit really took them.

As Springsteen explained in an interview with Sound published in March 1974 just as the album was released in Britain: *"There was more of the band in there and the songs were written more in the way that I wanted to write. But I tend to change the arrangements all the time in order to present the material best... for instance 'Sandy'. I like the way it is on the record but it was entirely different up until the night I recorded it and then I changed it."*

He added: *"The mistake is when you start thinking that you are your*

songs. To me a song is a vision, a flash, and what I see is characters and situations. I mean I've stood around carnivals at midnight when they're clearing up (as on 'Wild Billy's Circus Story') and I was scared, I met some dangerous people. As for Spanish Johnny's situation (in 'Incident On 57th Street')... I know people who have lived that life."

He described his new band as *"a real spacey bunch of guys"* and talked of his wish to perform in Britain. But doubted it would be soon, the US touring schedule taking such a bite out of his time. *"It just goes on forever here, on and on."*

With his reputation as a live performer growing with every fiery performance, even though it shared its predecessor's disappointing performance in the charts, 'The Wild, The Innocent and The E Street Shuffle' saw Springsteen and the E Street Band set out on what would be their most groundbreaking US tour yet. Critical plaudits were now starting to pile up. One notice, in particular, however, would capture the imagination of all who saw it, building in resonance throughout the years to become the most oft-recalled epithet of Springsteen's long career.

Jon Landau, who had given a largely glowing review to 'The Wild, The Innocent...' in 'The Real Paper', the local arts magazine he edited in Cambridge, Massachusetts, was also the 26-year-old reviews editor of 'Rolling Stone'. A music journalist who had already won the respect of the music industry by actually working in it as occasional producer and A&R man – he had produced the second MC5 album, 'Back In The USA' and championed Maria Muldaur's breakthrough hit 'Midnight At The Oasis' – although he had not been familiar with Springtseen's work previously, he was intrigued enough by his second album to go along and check him out when he played at local club, Charley's, in April 1974.

The timing of Landau's arrival at his first Springsteen show was prescient. Not only was the band reaching its musical apotheosis after playing together on the road solidly for over a year, but Bruce himself was fast evolving into the consummate live performer we know today; introducing songs with little autobiographical vignettes which served to both explain and frame the songs he sang. A livewire one moment, quiet and contemplative the next, and backed by a band entirely simpatico both musically and personally, Landau was knocked out by what he saw that night. So much so that when Bruce and the band returned to Cambridge for a follow-up date a month later – opening for Bonnie Raitt at the Harvard Square Theatre – Landau made sure he had a front-row seat. Once again, he was astounded by what he saw. Raitt had allowed the young pretender to perform his full two-hour show and Landau left that night even more convinced of this newcomer's unbelievable talent. It also happened to be the night of the critic's 27th birthday and when he settled down a few nights later to pen his review, Landau concluded: *"I saw my rock'n'roll past flash before my eyes. And I saw something else. I saw rock'n'roll's future and its name is Bruce Springsteen."*

Landau had plenty more to say in his review. *"Springsteen does it all"*, he wrote. *"He's a rock'n'roll punk, a Latin street poet, a ballet dancer, an actor, a poet joker, a bar band leader, hot-shit rhythm guitar player, extraordinary singer and a truly great rock'n'roll composer... he parades in front of his all-star rhythm band like a cross between Chuck Berry, early Bob Dylan and Marlon Brando. Every gesture, every syllable adds something to his ultimate goal – to liberate our spirit while he liberates his by baring his soul through his music."*

Yet it was that one telling phrase – *"I saw rock'n'roll's future and its name is Bruce Springsteen"* – that was destined to become the most oft-repeated quote of Springsteen's career. Columbia were quick to see the possibilities and immediately began running ads in all the music press for the new album, purloining Landau's memorable phrase. A judgement guaranteed to be seen by other critics as the throwing of a hat into the ring, by the time the UK music press had picked up on it, the line had turned into the less accurate but even more memorable: *"I have seen the future of rock'n'roll and its name is Bruce Springsteen."* Or simply: *"Bruce Springsteen is the future of rock'n'roll."* Naturally, there were those who found such sentiments ill-conceived, at best, downright scabrous at worst, and immediately set about proving Landau's theory wrong. With only the admirably written and played but woefully under-produced second album to go on, most British critics pooh-poohed the whole idea, and Springsteen was suddenly in danger of being written off as just another record company 'hype' – about the worst crime any young singer-songwriter wishing to be taken seriously could be accused of in those days.

Right or wrong, above all, Landau's proclamation had the effect of raising the bar of critical expectation for whatever Springsteen did next. From here on in, whatever he did, be it a concert tour, new album, or even just an interview, it would no longer be enough for him merely to be 'good'. As the official 'future of rock'n'roll' whatever he did next would always have to be great. It was now the least expected of him. As such, Landau's heartfelt but unbridled enthusiasm became a cross the young singer would have to bear for the rest of his career.

The question was: after an introduction like that, how would he ever be able to live up to it? The answer would come with his next album; the one he was telling friends he'd already decided to call 'Born To Run'.

Bruce Springsteen *Glory Days - 50 Years of Dreaming*

Chapter One

Chapter Two

Despite the mounting critical debate sparked by Jon Landau's review, by the summer of 1974 Bruce Springsteen was flat broke. Neither of his first two albums had sold well enough to even scratch the charts, much less pay the rent, and he was now deliberately thinking about how to make a radio-friendly hit single, in order to attract people's attention to the next album, which he was beginning to see as make or break for his career.

"We're at the lowest we've ever been right now", Bruce told Zigzag in August 1974. "Right now, we've just come off the road and the guys are getting thrown out of their houses. Hopefully I'll be getting some money from Columbia and maybe with David Bowie doing some of the songs ('Growin' Up' and 'It's Hard To Be A Saint In The City', neither of which would actually surface on a Bowie album for more than 20 years) that'll be good. But that's the only problem right now... I'd just like to be a little more secure that's all."

His first two albums, he conceded, had been "very different – the second is more popular and it's sold more. I guess it's more musical, but the first one has a certain something for me – the first album was a very radical album whereas the second wasn't quite so much. I'm surprised it didn't do better than it did because it sounded very commercial to me."

His next album, he predicted, would be "something of a balance between the two". He had already "written a lot of stuff – but it's a different assortment of material and most of it relates pretty much not to touring or playing in a band, because we haven't played much at all this summer. But lately I've been getting a rush to write new songs and I've got quite a few, some short and some long."

As it transpired, the third Springsteen album would be less a cross between his first two and far more a completely new take on everything he had tried to achieve up until then. Although he had already begun recording again at 914 Studios in New York, for some reason the vibe was simply not there this time, he and the band immediately getting bogged down on the song that would become the title track itself – an anthemic piece of widescreen fiction he called 'Born To Run'.

The song itself had been written on piano some months before. As Springsteen explained in a Mojo interview in 2006, "I'd written the lyrics sitting on the edge of my bed in this shack in Long Branch, New Jersey, thinking, "Here I come, world!" I did all the songs (on the album) on piano. They're filled with that tension of somebody trying to get some other place."

Nevertheless, he and the band struggled for a long time to get it right and several re-recordings were made over the following months. As guitarist Steve Van Zandt, an old friend of Bruce's but at the time, a new recruit to the studio band, recalled in the same piece: "Bruce knew exactly what he wanted and he wasn't going to stop until he got it. He had this brilliant vision of marrying the past with the future and he had this song which summed up the entire rock'n'roll experience. But the first two albums had been done more live, more spontaneous, and hadn't satisfied him, so maybe he thought he should try more modern methods."

This resulted in a painstaking process by which every instrument was recorded separately, building a musical mosaic, layer after layer. But Springsteen became frustrated and would often strip things back and make the band do it all again – and again. When, in the autumn of 1974, pianist David Sancious and drummer Ernest 'Boom' Carter (who had recently replaced Vini Lopez) left after being offered their own record deals, it seemed like the writing was on the wall. But the band soon steadied again with the arrival of keyboardist Roy Bittan and drummer Max Weinberg. Clarence Clemons: "I felt, what the hell's going on? But Roy and Max joined (and) they were fine by me."

Progress, albeit slowly, began to be made at last. Once again, however, it was Jon Landau who somehow managed to be the catalyst to the album's eventual success, chastising Bruce on a visit to 914 for working in such a small, under-equipped studio. "I said, "You're a big-league artist, you should be in a big-league studio." " Taking his words to heart, in April 1975 Springsteen moved the operation out of 914 and into the more hi-tech environs of the Record Plant. At which point he made what would prove to be the shrewdest move of his career thus far when he invited the ever more vocal Landau to work with him on the project as joint-producer. "One of my production ideas was that the sound would be tighter if we cut the record initially as a trio, just bass, drums and piano."

This they did and the results were immediate. Songs like 'Born To Run' and 'Tenth Avenue Freeze-Out' that had stubbornly refused to come together at 914 now began to gel and make sparks. Work continued throughout June and July of 1975. Clemons: "Some of it did come easily. 'The Night', for instance, that

Chapter Two

was, you feel it, you do it." Landau: "The last thing we did was the sax solo on 'Jungleland'. One little phrase at a time for 16 hours." Clemons: "I had to go to the bathroom a few times (but) I've had people say to me, "That sax solo saved my life." So I did my job." Springsteen: "' 'Born To Run' had become a monster... It just ate up everyone's life. At the end, I hated it. I thought it was the worst piece of garbage I'd ever heard." Needless to say, over 30 years later, he has revised his opinion somewhat. "When I hear the record now I hear my friends and I hear my hopes and dreams – a blessed part of my working life."

Eventually released in November 1975, 'Born To Run' immediately put Bruce Springsteen into rock's premier league. Given the tremendous hype that preceded its appearance, the critics were not so universally in favour this time but there was no doubt in the minds of the top brass at Columbia Records that this was by far the best thing their boy had ever done. Jon Landau's presence in the studio had helped steer the music towards the kind of grandiose Phil Spector wall-of-sound effect that perfectly matched Springsteen's starry-eyed romanticism and lavish arrangements, while the E Street Band had never sounded so cohesive, so together, so completely in control and on top of their game.

The overall theme of the album – whether emanating from the sparse piano-and-harmonica backing of the atmospheric opening track, 'Thunder Road', or the full-blown kitchen-sink drama of the unforgettable title track – may not have been original but it was breathlessly expressed; a perfect encapsulation of rock'n'roll at its most mythic and moving, it's most enervating and uninhibited. This was teenage rebellion as James Dean might have expressed it had he been a singer not an actor: tearful yet brave; confused yet passionate; a cry in the dark for a world just out of reach; the sound of West Side Story a generation on. 'Meeting Across The River', one of the few reflective moments on the album, a baleful trumpet wailing like a police siren above the nighttime tenements, recalled earlier observational sketches like 'Does This Bus Stop At 82nd Street', only now, the inky outlines had been filled with colour. At nine minutes plus in length, the album closer 'Jungleland' was, both literally and metaphorically, the biggest statement-of-intent Springsteen had made since 'Lost In The Flood', only now, the music had finally caught up with the lyrics, Clemons' solo tearing at the bowels of the song like an iceberg through the steel hull of a mighty ocean-going liner. While tracks like 'Tenth Avenue Freeze-Out' and 'The Night' simply rocked and rolled with the kind of soul-baring strut that had made the band so popular live, yet which they had singularly failed to fully capture until now in the recording studio.

For Clarence Clemons, whose huge sax sound had so much to do with the musical language of the album and who would be pictured on the stark black-and-white cover standing next to a grinning Bruce, 'Born To Run' would remain his favourite Springsteen album. "It depicted the raw wildness of what

rock'n'roll is all about", he said. "It defines the rebelliousness, that's what I got out of it. Songs like 'The Night' are my favourites." As well as 'Jungleland', which he admitted he was particularly proud of, especially his own sax solo, "even if I do say so myself".

But if 'Born To Run' seemed to sum up everything Bruce Springsteen would come to represent, certainly in the minds of both his staunchest fans and critics, it was also the last album of its kind Springsteen would ever make. It was also around this time that his American fans began calling him The Boss – a fact he claims he has never been entirely comfortable with. As he later explained to Dave Di Martino in Creem, it was a name given to him initially by the people who worked for him. "Then somebody started to do it on the radio. It's funny, cos I hate being called 'Boss'. I just do. Always did, from the beginning. I hate bosses. I hate bein' called a boss. Everybody says "Hey Boss", and I say "No, Bruce, Bruce!" "

Nevertheless, it was an epithet that seemed to sum up his fans' feelings for an artist who had become more than just a denim-shirted brother-figure to them, but the patriarchal embodiment of everything they themselves dreamed of doing with their lives: hitting the road and finding escape, redemption even, somewhere out on the chrome-wheel, fuel-injected highway. But for Springsteen himself it represented a coming-of-age. The last time his music would ever sound so wide-eyed and innocent.

Within weeks of its appearance, 'Born To Run' had entered the US Top 10 – it eventually reached Number 3, becoming his first million-seller – and the record company hype-machine moved into serious gear, achieving the ultimate promotional coup de grâce when they engineered it so that Springsteen appeared simultaneously on the covers of both Time and Newsweek magazines in the same week – an unprecedented feat for a pop singer. The effect of this double whammy was double edged in the same way as Landau's previous 'rock'n'roll future' statement had been. It certainly caught the world's attention. It also attracted its fair share of disdain. Clemons later claimed he never even looked at the Time and Newsweek issues with Bruce on the cover. As the oldest member of the group, he already had a wife and family, had worked in normal jobs and just wasn't moved by the press hype, he claimed, seeing it for what it was. "I didn't have any time for any of that", he shrugged dismissively.

Nevertheless, the hype continued. When Springsteen arrived in London for his first ever British shows – two nights at the Hammersmith Odeon in October 1975 – the posters put up all over the city by his record company loudly proclaimed: "Finally London is ready for Bruce Springsteen!" Already wearied by the critical hubris such overblown statements caused, Bruce and the band went out before the first show and personally tore down as many of the posters as they could, but the campaign became a standing joke in the music business.

Bruce Springsteen Glory Days – 50 Years of Dreaming

As ever, Bruce took the jibes personally. As he would tell Richard Williams in the Sunday Times six years later, *"What my band and I are about is a sense of responsibility. If you accept that, it makes you responsible for everything that happens. People tend to blame circumstances, but in the end it's always your choice. Take Elvis. He lost control. After a while, he even lost control of his own body. Starting in 1975, I had to fight a battle to regain control of what I do."*

Meanwhile, back out on the road after his year spent grafting in recording studios, Bruce and the band were finally starting to enjoy themselves again. The two London shows may not have been received well by critics fighting to see through the hype – as their UK correspondent, Simon Frith, wrote in Creem, *"What the hype had done… was convince us that this was going to be the greatest live act of the '70s"*. Instead, he discovered a singer-songwriter *"wearing a woolly hat… and dirty baggy pants… like Dustin Hoffman being Ratso Rizzo in Midnight Cowboy! This is the future of rock'n'roll??"* he asked incredulously.

Elsewhere, however, Springsteen's shows were now being received with the kind of critical rapture that would become familiar over the next three decades. Reviewing the first of four nights that Springsteen performed at the legendary Roxy club in Los Angeles, in October 1975 – tickets for which were all sold the day they went on sale – Don Snowden, writing in the Pasadena Guardian, began shrewdly by describing 'Born To Run' as *"the best of mid-'60s music seen through the muddy filter of the '70s"*, before memorably concluding: *"As a singer, he was technically no great shakes. But as a vocal dramatist, he was a master, going from a hoarse stage whisper to a colourful whoop just where and when each song, each story, most needed it; his timing instinctual and rarely wrong; drawing on a blood-red imagery so vivid you needed sunglasses to read the lyric sheet sometimes. He may have been using the same old clichés as everyone else – girls, cars, the frustrations of being a boy in a man's body, ever-present dream of escape – but with an unusual level of intelligence and emotional intensity, almost cinematic in their scope, not found in the songs of others, even Dylan."*

By now, the E Street Band had solidified into: Mighty Max (drums), Garry W. Tallent (bass), Danny Federici (organ/accordion), Roy Bittan (piano), Miami Steve (guitar) and Big Man Clarence Clemons (saxophones). An imposing figure on stage, Clemons provided the much-needed presence and credibility that underpinned the whole performance, offering a proper balance between Springsteen's obvious sensitivity and Miami Steve's swaggering gangster cool. Certainly Springsteen was no longer alone in seeing what he did as important. As Van Zandt – who would go as far as having his marriage ceremony actually performed by the Reverend Little Richard – would later tell Bill Holdship in Creem, *"I think people are a little afraid of the power of rock'n'roll. It's a powerful form of communication… something that even governments and religion can't accomplish. Rock'n'roll's not going away. It's going to be bigger than ever, I think.*

It's going to be important again. It's been irrelevant for so many years that it's time for it to change again." He added: *"I just see apathy all around, and the hope we had in the '60s – that we were going to change the world – is gone. It just seems like all we learned was how to get high and go into a coma in the end."*

Everywhere they went the stars now turned out to see them. In LA in 1975 that meant an audience studded with famous faces, from Jack Nicholson and Robert de Niro to Gregg Allman and then girlfriend Cher, to Alice Cooper, Tom Waits, Jackson Browne, Jim Messina, Wolfman Jack, and many others almost as famous. The highlight of the show most nights now was not 'Born To Run', 'Thunder Road' or even 'Jungleland', but 'Kitty's Back', which had evolved into a 15-minute-plus jam, during which everyone in the band got to show off their musical chops. 'Rosalita' still closed the set in breakneck Latinate rock'n'roll style, Clemons chasing Springsteen around the stage; like two overgrown kids playing in the yard. Then there would be the encores, which could go on almost as long as the set itself some nights. Kicking off at the Roxy with a cover of the Byrds' 'Catch Me If You Can', more often than not Bruce would follow that with Mitch Ryder and the Detroit Wheels' 'Devil With A Blue Dress On' and Little Richards' 'Good Golly Miss Molly'. Depending on the mood, the band would then segue maybe into 'C.C. Rider' and a fistful of other old rock'n'roll classics. In LA, they also threw in a performance of 'Backstreets' so overwhelming it had one critic comparing it to 'Like A Rolling Stone' from Dylan's legendary 1966 performance at the Albert Hall. Whichever way the set moved, however, the finale was almost always an over-the-top version of Gary 'US' Bonds' 1960s hit, 'Quarter To Three'.

Each night, it seemed, the show just got longer and longer. As did the tour: originally scheduled to run for nine months, the 'Born To Run' world tour effectively ran for almost three years, as Springsteen criss-crossed America several times, as well as taking in first visits to Britain, Europe, Australia and Japan. *"I thought it would never end"*, Bruce said later. Nevertheless, he did everything in his power to try and keep at least one foot on the ground. Still on the road at the start of 1977, when the tour arrived in Memphis, Bruce decided he would like to meet Elvis Presley. But instead of getting the record company to call ahead and arrange a meeting as most stars might have done at that point, Bruce decided simply to go down to Presley's Graceland mansion and climb over a wall! Hardly the first fan of 'the King' to try such a thing, he was quickly apprehended by Elvis' security team, who had never heard of Bruce Springsteen. Informed that Presley was, in any case, in Las Vegas, where he was performing, the recalcitrant young singer was sent packing with a flea in his ear.

Less fancifully, Springsteen's newfound success forced him to take stock of his own now vastly improved position in the music business, at which point he made important decisions. Unlike his record company, who urged him to hurry up and get back in the studio to make what they fervently hoped would be the 'sequel' to 'Born To Run', Bruce decided his next album would have to be as different as he could make it from its immensely popular predecessor. He also decided he needed a new manager, and that he had gone as far as he could in his career with Mike Appel at the helm. Instead, he offered the job to Jon Landau; the man who had started the critical ball rolling with his 'rock'n'roll future' review, then put his money where his mouth was by rolling up his sleeves and actually helping out in the studio.

Understandably, Appel did not take the news well and immediately instigated legal proceedings; action that would lead to many months and eventually years in court before the whole matter was finally settled. Avoiding press interviews, Bruce filled in the time writing songs for other artists, most notably fellow New Jersey-ite Southside Johnny, punk-poetess Patti Smith (giving Smith her biggest hit with 'Because The Night') and Robert Gordon (who also hit big with 'Fire'). When he wasn't doing that, he was writing his next album – what would be the most studious piece of work since his first album; a bleak yet beautiful masterpiece he had already decided to call 'Darkness On The Edge Of Town'. Recorded over a nine-month period with Landau once again co-piloting at the studio controls, and finally released in June 1978, the aptly titled 'Darkness On The Edge Of Town' found Bruce Springsteen in much more sombre mood than any recording he had made previously. Featuring a cast of characters whose motives were cloudier than any had been before, almost all of whom would be thrown into increasingly desperate situations, tracks like 'Badlands' and 'Racing In The Streets' still somehow managed to lend a certain dignity and appeal to the misfits whose stories they told, further establishing Springsteen as the most masterful chronicler of small-town American life to emerge in the 1970s.

Despite the baleful nature of its contents, 'Darkness...' still made the Top 5 in the US album charts and the Top 10 in the UK, where it became his most critically revered album yet. As Paul Rambali wrote in the NME, 'Promotion this time is distinctly low profile. The budget has been limited by his order, and no words of hyperbole adorn the ads – just 'Bruce Springsteen, his new album'. And in the mighty opening rush of 'Badlands' you feel – if nothing else – it's good to have him back. The first South side cadence; the cavernous guitar sound; Clarence Clemons' rasping sax solo; the chord changes: it's a rousing textbook Springsteen anthem – as is its counterpart on the second side, 'The Promised Land'.

Four lines in and he squares up to the events that have overtaken him since the release of 'Born To Run': "*I'm caught in a crossfire that I don't even understand*"... The blockbuster production techniques of 'Born To Run' have been studiously avoided, and the conquer-the-world romantic of before sounds oddly disillusioned, frustrated even.'

Bruce Springsteen Glory Days – 50 Years of Dreaming

Chapter Two

Bruce Springsteen *Glory Days - 50 Years of Dreaming*

A point Mitchell Cohen in Creem also picked up on, describing the album as *"an artful, passionate, rigorous record that walks a slender line between defeat and defiance"*. Before adding, *"But if frustration is its subject... it's also its essence, its soul. The best of this music – 'Badlands', 'Streets Of Fire' – doesn't just describe the rage, it embodies it... the album is about as powerful as rock'n'roll gets."*

One thing everyone agreed on was that the songs on 'Darkness...' found Springsteen developing the sort of story-telling songwriting he had begun previously with songs like 'Does This Bus Stop At 82nd Street' and 'Meeting Across The River' – most obviously, in this instance, on tracks like the seven-minute opus, 'Racing In The Street', which appeared to deal head-on with the line of criticism that insisted he was merely a glorified 'cars-and-girls' writer, and not least the brooding title track itself, a typically widescreen evocation of all the themes the album seems to explore – father-and-son conflict, Catholic guilt and confusion, the disappointment that growing up inevitably brings, when you discover there are no answers, just more complicated questions...

Thankfully, the album did offer up occasional lighter moments, as on 'Prove It All Night', an upbeat get-the-girl song that also served as the first single. Mainly, though, the album concerns itself with uncompromising fare like 'Adam Raised A Cain', a moody slow-burner, 'Factory', about what it must have been like for his father to spend his precious days working his knuckles to the bone, and 'Candy's Room', a song, quite simply, about what it's like to find yourself in love with a whore. Occasionally, as on 'Something In The Night' or 'Streets Of Fire', the tragic self-absorption and claustrophobic musical backdrop – prison-yard harmonica, chattering drums, clanging guitars and that occasionally intrusive, sax – teeter precariously close at times to overweening self-parody. But perhaps that's the price you pay when you attempt to bare your soul so completely.

Certainly, if Springsteen's overriding wish had been to avoid making 'Born To Run II', he had succeeded on every level. As Dave Di Martino later observed in Creem, *"What made 'Darkness...' so great, ultimately, was the sheer durability of its sentiment. The emotions dealt with on that set – loss, pain and despair – have always been the most durable, especially when they're conveyed as well and as meaningfully as Springsteen surprisingly managed... (His fans) loved it. But they would've loved 'Born To Run Part Two' even more."*

Out on the road, too, the shows became less celebratory, more intimate, even, paradoxically, as the venues grew bigger. But by then it hardly mattered. Bruce Springsteen was no longer operating at the same critical altitude as most of his contemporaries. For if 'Born To Run' had made him a superstar, 'Darkness On The Edge Of Town' had transformed him into something even more alluring: he was now an artist; a saint; a messiah. Wherever he went now and whatever he did next, he would have the world's full attention.

Chapter Two

Chapter Three

If 'Darkness On The Edge Of Town' had confounded all expectations, Bruce Springsteen's next album, 'The River', released in October 1980, seemed designed to please everybody. A double album containing over 83 minutes of music on 20 tracks, it was, in many ways, an encapsulation of everything he had stood for as an artist up until that point – from the vexed solipsism of '...Asbury Park' and 'Darkness...' to the more upbeat, full-swing bravado of 'The Wild, The Innocent...' and 'Born To Run'. In the sweeping title track, 'The River', the album also signposted one of the less expected ways in which Springsteen would move his career with his next album, the all-acoustic 'Nebraska'.

But that was still two years and many thousands of road miles away and the overriding impression the fifth Bruce Springsteen album left on listeners in 1980 was of an artist at the very height of his considerable powers; prolific to the point of saturation, there really did seem to be at least two different albums' worth of material on 'The River'. So much so that in retrospect, many critics would argue that a stripped-down single version of 'The River' would have produced perhaps the greatest album of Springsteen's career. Certainly, when one considers the claims of at least eight of the tracks to all-time greatness, it is a point worth considering. Ultimately, however, the worst that could be said of the remaining 12 tracks was that they were merely very good, missing out on true greatness by only a notch or two.

Perhaps over-compensating for the unforgiving nature of so much of the doom-laden material on 'Darkness...' one of the most instantly appealing features of 'The River' was its re-emphasis of the influence of the never-less-than-superb E Street Band, who can be heard stomping and whooping it up on a number of delightful tracks, from the Stonesy 'Crush On You' to the slick 1950s sheen of 'Sherry Darling' and 'Cadillac Ranch' – or, best of all, 'Hungry Heart', the most enervating slice of pure rock and soul Bruce had written for the band since 'Born To Run', full of joyously pumping piano, honking sax and a gloriously catchy chorus.

Tracks like 'Drive All Night', meanwhile, are full of the same foreboding that ran like a bleak seam through 'Darkness...'. As are the similarly dark and shadowy 'Stolen Car' and 'Wreck On The Highway'. Springsteen would confess that this had been a quite deliberate ploy on his part, to try and reintroduce some of the lightness of touch and sheer sense of fun that had been missing from 'Darkness...'. Most of the *"serious stuff"*, he revealed, had been written in 1979, when 'The River' was still being viewed as a regular-sized single album, with almost all the lighter moments being added in 1980, once Springsteen had actually begun recording – which was when the idea of turning it into a double-album first took hold. The long wait between 'The River' and 'Darkness...', he further explained, was down to the fact that he'd taken so much care trying to get the album right, figuring that as he'd be playing the songs for at least the next six months, he had better make sure he liked what he was playing. That said, he still insisted that he had never done more than ten takes of any of the songs, most of them, in fact, being completed in far less. All in all, he said, he had actually recorded somewhere in the region of 40 tracks, from which the final 20 were eventually chosen.

With so many tracks to wade through, so many new characters and stories to get to know, the sheer scope of the songs hinted at the novel the album might have been had Springsteen been a conventional author rather than a singer, full of nuanced details and emotional gasps. At times, as on the ponderous 'The Price You Pay', the effect could be overly serious, perhaps, and simply too wearing. At its best, though, as on the emotional title track itself or the hymn-like 'Independence Day' (yet again, about escaping home and leaving his father behind), or most affecting of all, on something like the effortlessly haunting 'Wreck On The Highway', the lyrics worked almost like a three-act play. As a singer, he had also found a new depth to his voice. Where once he might have angrily implored, now he simply told the story as a mature observer, not so much outside the story as simply beyond.

As Bruce would explain to Dave Di Martino of Creem in January 1981, *"When I did 'Darkness...' I was very focused on one particular idea, one particular feeling that I wanted to do... I just didn't make room for certain things, ya know? Because I couldn't understand how you could feel so good and so bad at the same time. And it was very confusing for me. 'Sherry Darling' was gonna be on 'Darkness...', 'Independence Day' was a song that*

Bruce Springsteen *Glory Days – 50 Years of Dreaming*

Chapter Three

was gonna be on 'Darkness...', and the song that I wrote right after 'Darkness' was 'Point Blank' – which takes that thing to its furthest."

Or as Phil Sutcliffe noted in his October 1980 review for Sound, *"Compare Springsteen's performance on 'The River' with 'Darkness...' and you find a huge shift. Where Springsteen used to run bare-naked through his emotions now he wears a sober suit. He's been over the top, he knows he can do that. This time it seems he wanted to see whether he could tear it apart quietly. Brave again. Restraint might have called his bluff, exposed him as just plain noisy rather than soulful. It didn't."*

Sutcliffe concluded his review in suitably melodramatic style: *"I emerge from a weekend with this record feeling as my parents did when they'd survived the blitz. Tattered and frayed round the edges and yet with a glow for man and womankind which might lead to dangerous excursions like embracing someone I've never met before. Springsteen and the E Street Band have that quality of making you feel more alive – because, I'm convinced, you actually are more open and aware after allowing such music inside you. 'The River' is as good as blood."*

Not everybody was so smitten, however. According to Ira Robbins, in Trouser Press, 'The River' was *"buried in an avalanche of repetition and evident lack of inspiration. Like a painter with a monochromatic palette, Springsteen is limited to working with his too-familiar 'street' character. As a result, his undynamic [sic] new tracks lack both the urgency and clarity of past successes. Instead of impact or emotional urgency, Springsteen substitutes a ridiculous 'party atmosphere'. 'The River' adds up to a water-treading exercise that neither upholds his standards of excellence nor explores any new avenues... Out of 20 tracks, 13 use 'night'; nine use 'street' and there are four with 'highway' and two with 'avenue'; 'drive' turns up in ten songs, as does 'heart'. And these few words appear constantly throughout many of his previous songs as well. Repetitive language might be forgivable if the songs dealt with different subjects, but Springsteen just goes back over the same ground, neither refining nor elucidating — merely restating."*

It was the Sound review that most of his growing legion of fans seemed to agree most with, though, and the Springsteen camp celebrated in style when 'The River' quickly went to Number 1 in the US charts – the first Springsteen album ever to do so, and an even more amazing feat considering it was a more expensively-priced double-album at that.

Touring America now, he was playing only the largest arenas; arriving onstage at 8.00pm with no support act. It was also the first time the chants of *"Bruuuce! Bruuuuce!"* began; sounding somewhere between a boo and a howl but signalling the kind of unrestrained adoration few other artists have ever known. Bruce in tight black T-shirt and cowboy boots – still looking like the older, more complicated brother of James Dean, still

Bruce Springsteen Glory Days – 50 Years of Dreaming

Chapter Three

unconsciously mixing Elvis with Dylan – was now leading his extraordinary band through four-hour shows split into two halves – just like a Broadway musical – with the new songs from 'The River' making up just half of the first half of the show and only some of the second half. Most of the onstage tomfoolery now seemed choreographed too, so used had his fans become to the mugging between Bruce the white boy and Clarence Clemens, his Big Black Brother. Clicking his fingers during the opening verses of 'I'm On Fire' a light would pop into his hand; introducing a song with another one of his 'impromptu' stories, regular visitors to the tour knew what was coming almost word-for-word some nights. Like the one that went, *"I remember when I was nine years old and I was sittin' in front of the TV set and my mother had Ed Sullivan on and on came Elvis. I remember right from that time, I looked at her and I said, "I wanna be just... like... that". But I grew up and I didn't want to be just like that no more. Because he was like the biggest dreamer. He was like a big liberator. I remember I was sittin' at home when a friend of mine called and told me that he died, which wasn't that big a surprise at the time because I'd seen him a few months earlier in Philadelphia. I thought a lot about it – how somebody could've had so much, could in the end lose so bad and how dreams don't mean nothin' unless you're strong enough to fight for 'em and make 'em come true. You gotta hold on to yourself."*

It was also on this tour that Bruce began the practice of having female fans join him onstage for some 'impromptu' dancing, topped off with a kiss before being gently led away into the wings by the roadies (a moment immortalised five years later in the video for 'Dancing In The Dark'). But if his onstage moves were now becoming familiar, a trademark, the spontaneity of the set-list – the sheer unbridled joy of the music – more than made up for that, rocking unselfconsciously through showstoppers like 'Sherry Darling' or 'Two Hearts' one moment, then slowing everything down and delivering an emotional coup de grâce on 'The River', the new highlight of the set, delivered early in the first half of the show.

Once again, the world tour would take in America, Canada, Britain, Europe, Japan and Australia. At the first date of the tour in Michigan, however, he rather embarrassingly forgot some of the words to Born To Run' and had to ask the audience to prompt him. He had less trouble with the rest of the set, though, which now included established hits like 'Prove It All Night', 'Tenth Avenue Freeze-Out', a hyperemotional 'Darkness On The Edge Of Town', a sparse and eerie 'Thunder Road', followed by the equally barnstorming 'Badlands'.

The second half of the show would usually kick-off with a feverish 'Cadillac Ranch', followed by 'Fire', the song he wrote for Robert Gordon but always did so much better himself. From there the set would continue to build through showstoppers like 'Hungry Heart' and 'You Can Look (But You Better Not Touch)'. It would often be after midnight before they even got around to thinking about the encores, which usually began with 'Rosalita', replete with a fake slow intro to tease the crowd; 'Jungleland' with Bruce and Clarence – who the singer was now introducing onstage every night as *"the next president of the United States!"* – coming at it from opposite sides of the stage; then the 'Devil In The Blue Dress' Detroit-medley familiar from previous tours, the whole shebang ending some four hours after it had begun with 'Quarter To Three'.

According to the promoters, the whole 43-date US tour had sold-out within hours of going on sale – on the strength of a simple radio announcement, which included snatches of his songs but no actual mention of his name – with mail-order applications alone accounting for more than 200,000 ticket sales just in New York! The four nights he also sold out at the Sports Arena in Los Angeles left ticketless fans reportedly paying up to $100 per seat. Meanwhile, back home in New Jersey, he was booked to perform at the inaugural concert of a new 20,000-seater stadium and 'Born to Run' had been adopted as the state's official anthem. Even though his last major American shows had been nearly two years before, this was still an unprecedented level of demand for a performer who had been struggling to pay the rent just five years before. As he explained to Creem in January 1981, *"We're gonna be playing a lot of shows, and we're just gonna be out there for a real long time. And when I go out there at night, I just like to feel... like myself. And like I've done what I have to do. And when I play those songs onstage, I know those songs, I know what went into 'em and I know where I stand. And people will like it and people will not like it, but I know that it's real. I know that it's there."*

Even the previously taciturn British critics now saw new layers of meaning in the Springsteen live extravaganza. Reviewing his show at the Brighton Centre for 'Melody Maker', in May 1981, Lynden Barber gushed: *"When Springsteen's up there on stage, a lifetime's hopes, passions and frustrations explode in an uninhibited cry matched only by the sense of exhilaration and freedom a mountaineer must feel on reaching the summit. And if at times Springsteen strays too near the edge and stumbles down the slopes towards sentimentality, it's a mistake that's dwarfed by the magnitude of his overall achievement."* The review concluded: *"Since the concert, I've realised that 'The River' is not An Album in the same sense as 'Born To Run' or 'Darkness On The Edge Of Town', but should be seen as a record that closely follows the dynamics of a live Springsteen show; an epic that balances the hedonistic joy of rock with the more complex exploration of the human emotions that characterised earlier songs like 'Badlands' and 'The Promised Land'... the power of Bruce and the E Street Band on stage is* enough to move even the emotionally crippled."

A similarly passionate view of the UK shows that year was expressed in the Sunday Times by the redoubtable Richard Williams, who wrote of *"a synthesis of rock's greatest strengths"* that could be found in Springsteen's music: *"Presley's snarl, the romance of The Drifters, Phil Spector's grandiose mini-symphonies, the drive of The Rolling Stones and the social awareness of the punks…".* Williams went on to report how more than 300,000 people had applied to promoter Harvey Goldsmith's office for the 105,000 available tickets. An amazing feat considering that by the time of his 1981 shows – his first in the UK since the two Hammersmith shows in 1975 – Springsteen had never even had a hit single in Britain. When the writer caught up with the singer just before his first ever Wembley Arena show, however, he found a man less concerned with money and statistics and more interested in discussing the real motivation behind his success: the same thing, in fact, that lay at the heart of his most popular songs: escape; freedom; choice; potential.

"My father was a pretty good pool-player, and not much else," he said. *"When he was about the age I am now (31), he was offered a job with the telephone company, but he turned it down because it would have meant travelling away from his wife and kids. Years later, I realised how that missed opportunity had hurt him ever since. So I've always felt that if you're fortunate enough to be up there on stage, it's your responsibility to try and close the gap with the audience, to give them the sense that there are other possibilities than the ones they may be seeing."* He concluded: *"Being in a band and playing music is what got me out of the trap of never realising my potential."* He was now being bootlegged so regularly that, where once he had seen the circulation of unofficial live albums of his shows as a backhanded compliment, he now began to take umbrage at the millions of dollars allegedly being made by the pirates from a vast array of illicit recordings, from live radio performances, to rehearsal tapes, outtakes of recording sessions and more. A series of court actions were taken out to try and stem the flow. They didn't, but Bruce had made his point, he felt, to the Springsteen fans: that he did not endorse such releases, and in most cases actively fought them, seeing them as inferior products he would never have put his name to ordinarily. But when this still did not work, he announced his intention to put out his own official live album, comprised of recordings taken largely from 'The River' world tour but also earlier tours. *"The people who were doing it had warehouses full of records, and they were just sittin' back gettin' fat – putting out anything and getting 30 fuckin' dollars for it",* he complained. *"And I just got really mad about it."*

Meanwhile, the critical plaudits were now seriously piling up. Even Greil Marcus, a veritable institution in American rock journalism – and renowned Dylanologist – now waded in with his own fresh critique on the burgeoning Springsteen phenomenon, writing in New West magazine in 1981: *"As songwriter, singer, guitarist and bandleader, (Bruce Springsteen) appears at once as the anointed successor to Elvis Presley and as an impostor who expects to be asked for his stage pass. His show is, among other things, an argument about the nature of rock'n'roll after 25 years. The argument is that rock'n'roll is a means to fun that can acknowledge the most bitter defeats, that it has a coherent tradition which, when performed, will reveal possibilities of rock'n'roll the tradition did not previously contain."* He went on: *"It means that at his finest Springsteen can get away with almost anything, stuff that coming from anyone else would seem hopelessly corny and contrived – and that he can come up with stuff to get away with that most rockers since Little Richard would be embarrassed even to have thought of."*

Motivated perhaps by this ever more penetrating critical spotlight, Springsteen again found himself reaching deep within when the time arrived for him to begin working on material for his next album in 1982. Having dropped out of school early and, by his own admission, never having really been comfortable holding a book in his hand, Springsteen began addressing what he now, in his thirties, saw as this glaring gap in his education, picking up and reading as much literature as he could. Aided in his reading by the suggestions of the former college graduate, Jon Landau, Bruce found himself wading through volumes of American history, alongside the semi-biographical works of such giants of American letters as John Steinbeck, whose Grapes Of Wrath proved to be a particular favourite.

As Springsteen confided to an audience in Paris in 1981, *"I was lucky… because I met this guy (Landau) when I was in my middle 20s, who said you should watch this (film) or you should read this (book). And most people, where I come from, never have someone try and help them in that way. So all I'm sayin' is, is try and learn, learn about yourselves, learn about who you are now. And try and make it better for who's gonna be comin'. Because the real future of rock'n'roll's only about nine years old today…"*

As a result of his manager's informal tutelage, it was also around this time that he happened to alight upon a book by the famed Vietnam veteran Ron Kovic, an autobiography evocatively titled, Born On The 4th Of July (later to be made into the Oscar-nominated movie of the same name starring Tom Cruise). As chance would have it, Springsteen had not long finished reading the book when he was actually introduced to Kovic in Los Angeles. Their ensuing friendship would lead directly to Bruce's involvement in such fund-raising joint-ventures as the Vietnam Veterans Of America organisation, formed to give a voice and support to the many thousands of ex-military men and women now disenfranchised by an America that preferred to forget about Vietnam and/or view the whole debacle as a shameful episode in American history to be ranked alongside the Watergate presidential scandal and the assassination of JF Kennedy. For those brave and unfortunate conscripts who had no choice in the matter, Vietnam was not an experience so easily brushed beneath the carpets of history and, inspired by Kovic and his own father's sometimes bitter army memories, Springsteen now involved himself in as much "community involvement", as he reasonably could. As a result, Springsteen would shackle almost all his subsequent tours in the 1980s to raising publicity and/or personal donations to a range of domestic and international causes, from aiding American food banks to supporting the long-suffering wives of striking English miners in Newcastle-upon-Tyne.

Needless to say, it wasn't long before his newfound commitments were reflected in his songwriting too. The first and most important example of this was when, on January 3, 1982, he sat down at his rented house in Holmdel, New Jersey, and began writing and roughly recording more than a dozen new songs onto a four-track TEAC tape-recorder. The initial idea had been simply to produce a set of demos that he and the E Street Band would later work up into 'finished' album tracks. When, however, almost all of the tracks seemed to fall apart under the strain of a full band blasting them out, he began to toy with the idea of simply leaving them as they were – acoustic, recorded solo at home, just him and the long shadows for company. The end result was one of the most compelling albums of his career, 'Nebraska'.

If 'Nebraska' was a surprise to the fans, the band itself seemed to take this strange unexpected turn in the road with a degree of equanimity that did them proud. Drummer Max Weinberg best summed up their collective attitude to being told they wouldn't be on the next Springsteen album when he described his and the rest of the E Street Band's chief role as being there "to help Bruce with his vision", adding that he was "an extremely strong individual" and "the most patient person I ever met."

Perhaps his audience should have seen it coming on 'The River' tour when he began doing Woody Guthrie's call-to-arms for the lonely and dispossessed, 'This Land Is Your Land', but 'Nebraska' was about as far removed from the youthful glory-hunting of 'Born To Run' as it was possible to get. A radical departure from the rouged rock'n'roll of all his previous work, in fact, 'Nebraska' was an album whose stripped-back emotional fragility was as unexpected as it was astonishing. With just his own acoustic guitar and harmonica as musical accompaniment, Springsteen delved deep into previously unknown wells of loneliness and despair. If nothing else, 'Nebraska' also proved just how much the

simple strength of his songs actually underpinned the wall-of-sound the E Street Band had been developing all these years, and that it was, first and foremost, what he had to say – not how he said it – that made what he did so compelling.

Nowhere was this more convincingly demonstrated than on the track, 'State Trooper' – a harrowing exploration of the blurred boundaries between good and evil that so many ordinary people's lives represent, even those that would be seen as our guardians and peace-keepers. While the title track itself – from which the plot of the movie Natural Born Killers, made over a decade later, might easily have been taken – was so cold and world-weary-sounding it made you fear for the mental state of both the protagonist and his beyond-caring girlfriend. Murder is used here as metaphor but it still stank of someone else's blood. As Springsteen later explained in his introduction to the song on stage at the Shrine Auditorium, Los Angeles, in 1990, "This is a story about disconnection and isolation. I've always been fighting between feeling really isolated and looking to make some connection or find some community to belong to. I guess that's why I picked up the guitar initially. I spend enormous periods of time feeling very isolated. I guess this is a song about what happens when that side of you gets really set loose. And you don't feel the connections, and you don't feel what sense laws make or morality makes. And you're gone..."

Most tellingly, perhaps, where in the past the image of a fast car in a Bruce Springsteen song symbolised escape to a better possible world where love could be passionately expressed without fear of betrayal and heroes were ordinary guys in dirty sneakers and old jeans, the only cars in the songs on 'Nebraska' seemed to be heading down cold, empty roads leading to badly lit dead-ends and treacherous corners. Escape is no longer an option but an illusion enjoyed by people too young to know any better. Now approaching his mid-thirties, having seen all there was to see of the rock'n'roll dream, the singer knows that that is all it is, all it ever was – merely a dream. He had hinted at it before, of course, on songs like 'Wreck On The Highway', but here at last was the unvarnished truth, without the band there to add lustre at least to the sharp edge of his darkest observations. The story of 'Johnny 99', meanwhile, might have been the middle-aged sequel to that of the main characters in 'Born To Run' as Johnny finds himself in an ever-deepening spiral of depression and debt, made redundant from the car plant he has worked in all his married life, so hopeless he ends up killing an innocent man during a small-time robbery, for which the judge gives him 99 years in the jailhouse. Then there's that of the 'Highway Patrolman' who somehow finds himself driving through the hardest part of a long cold night to arrest his own brother, guilty of some nameless yet entirely understandable crime.

Bruce In Colour

Bruce In Colour

Bruce Springsteen *Glory Days – 50 Years of Dreaming*

Bruce In Colour

Bruce Springsteen *Glory Days - 50 Years of Dreaming*

Bruce In Colour

Bruce Springsteen *Glory Days — 50 Years of Dreaming*

Bruce In Colour

Bruce Springsteen *Glory Days - 50 Years of Dreaming*

Bruce In Colour

Bruce Springsteen *Glory Days – 50 Years of Dreaming*

Bruce In Colour

Bruce Springsteen *Glory Days – 50 Years of Dreaming*

Bruce In Colour

Bruce Springsteen *Glory Days - 50 Years of Dreaming*

Bruce In Colour

Bruce Springsteen *Glory Days – 50 Years of Dreaming*

Inspiration wasn't totally confined to social-historical observations, either. As he explained on stage to an audience in Minnesota, in June 1984, the lyrics to the track 'Mansion On The Hill' were inspired by a particularly vivid childhood memory, again involving his father. *"My father was always transfixed by money. He used to drive out of town and look at this big white house. It became a kinda touchstone for me. Now, when I dream, sometimes I'm on the outside looking in – and sometimes I'm the man on the inside."*

Even 'Reason To Believe', which seems initially to be about the possibility of redemption for all the losers-in-love and in-life that the rest of the album so powerfully evinces comes tinged with self-doubt and a barely contained fury. The only track on the entire album that appeared to offer up even a glimpse of light at the end of a very long tunnel was the deceptively throwaway 'Open All Night'. The record company feared The Boss may have over-estimated his audience's taste for such a bleak sounding soundscape and, while it was doubtless true that 'Nebraska' would not have pleased those that had merrily assumed they were in for another 'The River' or even 'Darkness On The Edge Of Town', its spiritual

forebear, 'Nebraska' garnered Springsteen some of the best, most thoughtful reviews of his career, which in turn brought with them a whole new audience, becoming a touchstone release along the way for a whole future generation of more musically homespun 'Americana' bands that would later appear on the scene in the mid-1990s.

Interestingly, one of the many songs that Springsteen omitted from 'Nebraska' was the first take of a song directly inspired by Kovic's own tale, entitled 'Born In The USA' – the same song (with a slightly different melody) which would become both the title track of his next full-band album and probably the most totemic song of his career – the original version of which would not be made available until 1998 on the 'Tracks' album, a fascinating collection of some of Bruce's outtakes over the years.

First though, would come the other, better-known version of the song that we all know now. At which point the Bruce Springsteen story would change all over again. So much so, in fact, nothing would ever be quite the same, for either him or his audience, again...

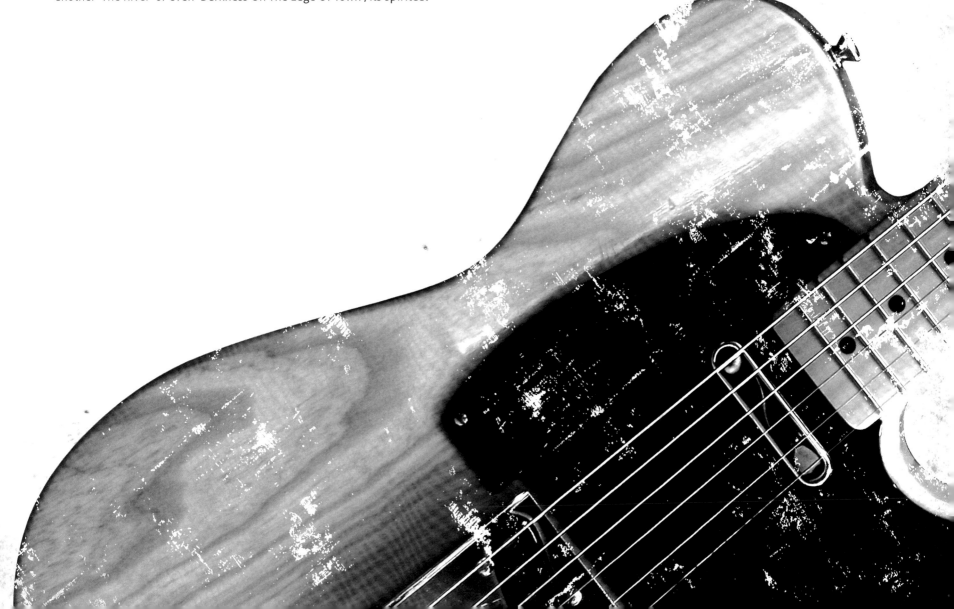

Chapter Four

I f the austere homespun folk-blues of the ghostly 'Nebraska' had stretched and altered the perception of Bruce Springsteen as an artist, demonstrating that there was more to him than a highly romanticised version of old-time '60s R&B mixed up with fuel-injected '50s-style rock'n'roll, its surprise follow-up in 1984, 'Born In The USA', appeared to almost bend over backwards in its attempt to redress the balance and prove that Springsteen belonged in the new streamlined, production-driven, image-conscious '80s as much as artists a decade younger.

'Born In The USA' would catapult Springsteen into the highest and mightiest echelons of mainstream rock. Bruce and the E Street Band had started recording material for Born In The USA in the first half of 1982. They continued, in bursts, over two years at New York's Power Station and Hit Factory studios, with Springsteen, Landau, Van Zandt and Chuck Plotkin co-producing and only two extra performers, backing vocalists La Bamba and Ruth Jackson, contributing to the tracks. They reputedly recorded 70 songs.

Brimming with rousing anthems and fiery rockers and the odd divine pop marvel, the finished album sounded so urgently, vividly commercial that it was possible to overlook its more serious content. As well as lingering over the troubles of small-town American citizens in his usual insightful and descriptive manner, Springsteen made a bolder statement. The sleeve's red, white and blue artwork and the lyrics of the title track made a direct attack on the American Government's foreign policy, the futility of the Vietnam war, and the shoddy treatment of homecoming soldiers.

Springsteen later commented, "I think the guy in 'Born In The USA' wants to strip away that mythic America which was Reagan's image of America. He wants to find something real and connecting. He's looking for a home in his country."

Ronald Reagan would be among those who got it wrong, mistaking the passionate chorusing for a declaration of patriotism. Campaigning during the 1984 Presidential election run-up, he stated, "America's future rests in a thousand dreams inside our hearts. It rests in the message of hope in the songs of a man that so many young people admire: New Jersey's own Bruce Springsteen."

New Jersey's own Bruce Springsteen faced similar problems night after night on the Born In The USA world tour when he played the song, every audience rising up to bellow loudly along and punch the air in a euphoric, mass celebration of America. Springsteen couldn't beat it, so he joined it, yelling out his words ever more vigorously, fist in the air like everybody else.

Released in June 1984, Born In The USA was an international Number One, selling in its millions. One of the biggest albums of the '80s, it set in stone Springsteen's image as a blue-jean blue-collar hero, stadium rock's own human Statue of Liberty, and it gave rise to seven Top 10 singles Stateside, beginning with 'Dancing In The Dark'.

The live-performance video was filmed over two days, firstly in front of a crowd of 200 extras and secondly – extraordinarily – at the opening night of the Born In The USA tour.

Audiences at the St Paul Civic Centre, Minnesota, on June 29th – the first of three nights at the venue – were treated to two renditions of 'Dancing In the Dark', one after the other, since director Brian De Palma needed a second take. And no one suspected that when Springsteen picked a pretty young girl out of the audience to come and dance onstage – an unsurprising thing for him to do – she was actually an actress planted there by De Palma.

Courtney Cox would later become rich and famous as the neurotic Monica in Friends.

The tour began without Steve Van Zandt, who had left the E Street Band to concentrate on the Disciples Of Soul. He wanted to become more overtly political than was possible with Springsteen – he would go on to form a campaigning musicians' alliance called Artists United Against Apartheid – although they remained great friends. Van Zandt's replacement was Nils Lofgren, an old acquaintance of Springsteen's. Lofgren had come to prominence in the '70s with a band called Grin, next playing with Neil Young's Crazy Horse and releasing albums in his own right. He talked to Sounds' Ralph Traitor about the E Street Band: "Just being a part of it, it's a real special treat that comes along, sometimes never, sometimes once in a lifetime... I have been a fan of his (Springsteen)

Chapter Four

for a long time, it's just personal taste, but I find myself laughing sometimes onstage because it's just such a great band."

Another new face on the stage was that of Patti Scialfa, a well-known New Jersey singer and a Stone Pony regular who had recorded with Southside Johnny & The Asbury Jukes and Tone, David Sancious's band, among others. Springsteen invited Patti to sing backing vocals on the Born In The USA tour, and as time went on, she assumed a more prominent position in the group, playing some acoustic guitar and creating a performing partnership with Bruce. (The partnership worked out so well that she eventually became Mrs. Springsteen, but not before he had married and divorced his first wife.)

In many places, the indoor arenas which had once seemed so big had given way to vast outdoor stadiums – in the UK, every show was a stadium gig – and the crowds grew wilder and noisier and more unpredictable. In Dallas, someone threw an artificial leg onto the stage. And in Vancouver and Dublin, there were dangerous scenes as fans stampeded towards the stage, trampling and crushing others as they charged.

Roy Bittan recalled, "*Being onstage was like being in the eye of the hurricane. There was a certain calmness there, while all around there was hysteria. While we all knew the tour had gotten very big and things were crazy like they'd never been before, I don't think the E Street Band really ever felt the full effects of it. The whole thing was dreamlike, because everyone's dreams were coming true. We all wanted to be in the biggest rock band in the world, and we were.*"

The entourage had expanded at the same rate as the venues. Now the band were surrounded by scores of industry employees, media hustlers, A-list stars and hangers-on, all bustling around, taking determined breaths of the same air as Bruce Springsteen.

The set lists this time were dramatically different to any that had gone before, for as well as the new material from Born In The USA, Springsteen was also playing selections from Nebraska for the first time. At St Paul Civic Centre on the opening night, he started out with 'Thunder Road' and proceeded as follows: 'Prove It All Night', 'Out In The Street', 'Johnny 99', 'Atlantic City', 'Mansion On The Hill', 'The River', 'No Surrender', 'Glory Days', 'The Promised Land', 'Used Cars', 'My Hometown', 'Born In The USA', 'Badlands', 'Hungry Heart', 'Dancing In The Dark' (twice), 'Cadillac Ranch', 'Sherry Darling', 'Highway Patrolman', 'I'm On Fire', 'Fire', 'Working On The Highway', 'Bobby Jean', 'Backstreets', 'Ramrod', 'Rosalita (Come Out Tonight)', 'I'm A Rocker', 'Jungleland', 'Born To Run', a cover of the Stones' 'Street Fighting Man' and 'Detroit Medley'.

The second and third nights in St Paul found Springsteen kicking off

with 'Born In The USA', as would be the case for almost all of the rest of the tour, sensibly: it made for an explosive and unforgettable entrance. During the early dates, he sometimes substituted 'Thunder Road' or 'Badlands' as the opener, and later on, there were one-off performances of 'High School Confidential' and an acoustic 'Independence Day' to start the set.

Predictably, he soon began working in other songs from Born In The USA and Nebraska, and from his wider back catalogue. 'No Surrender' quickly turned into an acoustic song rather than the full-band version heard at the early shows. Bruce played even fewer covers than he had on the River tour, and of those that did appear from time to time, only a few were making their first appearances. They included 'Wooly Bully', 'Can't Help Falling In Love', 'War' and 'When I Grow Up To Be A Man'. There was a novel amalgamation of 'Do You Love Me' with 'Twist And Shout', and the ever-changing 'Detroit Medley' widened its net yet again.

The bandana-wearing Springsteen looked different on this tour. He'd been working out, building muscles, developing a physique to match his musical stature and his maturity. The scrawny Jersey punk with the leather jacket and tight jeans and the big heart was a grownup now, with a physical, sexual presence that he confidently paraded onstage, shirtsleeves torn off to reveal his newly rippling biceps. And the new-look E Street Band took on an equally assured momentum.

This was an enormously potent rock show; some said the most powerful on the planet.

The tour included ten nights at New Jersey's Brendan Byrne Arena in August 1984, where the band received the tumultuous welcome of homecoming heroes and were joined at various performances by The Who's John Entwistle, Southside Johnny, Little Steven (Van Zandt) and the Miami Horns (who also took the stage in Philadelphia). On at least one of these evenings, Springsteen's parents were in the audience. In Oakland, California, on October 22nd, his sister Pam recreated the Courtney Cox role in 'Dancing In The Dark'. In January 1985, in Greensboro, North Carolina, Bruce was delighted to share his stage with both Gary US Bonds and his old Steel Mill co-vocalist Robbin Thompson for 'Twist and Shout'.

Little Steven was not a stranger. Following on from his Brendan Byrne spot, he popularly turned up to guest with the band in Memphis, Atlanta, London, Leeds and, finally, back in New Jersey during a four-night stint at the Meadowlands Giant's Stadium in August 1985 when the tour was approaching its conclusion. On the very last night, at the LA Coliseum on October 2nd, Springsteen's wife Julianne Philips – whom he married during the tour – took the spotlight with him in 'Dancing In The Dark',

Chapter Four

Bruce Springsteen *Glory Days - 50 Years of Dreaming*

and Jon Landau played guitar on the final encores of 'Rockin' All Over The World' and 'Glory Days'.

It had been a long, strange trip. Bruce Springsteen and the E Street Band had conquered new territories in Australia, Japan and Ireland just as capably as they'd stormed their existing strongholds all over again.

Whereas the key influences behind 'Nebraska' appeared to be a heady mixture of prime-time Woody Guthrie and early Bob Dylan, along with the biographical works of John Steinbeck and Ron Kovic, the chief influence on 'Born In The USA', on first acquaintance at least, appeared to be that of MTV, the new all-music video cable TV channel which had taken off in earnest in America just the year before. Even Springsteen's new, more clean-cut image – beardless for the first time since his teens, his pipe-cleaner arms suddenly rippling with muscles, his previously whip-thin body now filled out by what looked like regular sessions in the gym with a professional fitness trainer – seemed tailor-made to appeal to an audience that had now turned its back on the 1970s as the decade that taste forgot. An image reinforced by the album's iconic cover of the Boss dressed simply in a white T-shirt, blue jeans and a baseball cap set to a stars-and-stripes backdrop. Arriving as the album did, bang smack in the middle of the 1980s – post-AIDS, second-term Reagan – it was as if the Boss had gone out of his way to reinvent himself in a way previously thought impossible, let alone viable; anticipating the look of another soon-to-be-famous, yet ideologically entirely different, New Jersey rock star, Jon Bon Jovi, by a good two years.

And yet, while 'Born In The USA' appeared, superficially at least, to be a world away from the Bruce Springsteen his millions of fans had come to know and love, on closer inspection it soon became clear that much of the songs on it actually came from the same dark and desperate place as it's more obviously distressed predecessor. Indeed, the downtrodden characters that populated new songs like 'Downbound Train' might easily have been the very same that we had first been introduced to on the ultra bleak 'Nebraska'-era tracks like the harrowing 'Johnny 99'. Strip away the cacophonous sound of the E Street Band on 'Born In The USA', in fact, and you find what appears to amount to an anguished twin brother to 'Nebraska', no less. The other side of a coin, perhaps, that refuses to reflect the light whichever side faces it.

As the original acoustic version of it attests, the title track itself – its big drum-beating chorus instantly mistaken by less careful listeners for a pro-American, flag-waving rallying cry – was in fact the very opposite of what it appeared to be: a pain-filled howl of protest at the iniquities of the Vietnam War, aimed squarely at the way its messy, bungled aftermath had destroyed the lives of so many of its former participants and their

surrounding friends and families. It was a feeling, Springsteen later confessed, heightened by the fact that he himself had escaped the draft while so many of his childhood friends hadn't.

Somewhat amazingly, especially considering how impossible they had found trying to come up with electric versions of the other songs written during the same period – one of the main reasons why they ended up as solo acoustic performances on 'Nebraska' – the E Street Band blasted through 'Born In The USA' with such conviction that Bruce felt they had nailed it with just their second run-through in the studio, from the almighty thwack of Max Weinberg's huge snare drum, to Roy Bittan's unexpectedly shrill synthesizer riff, up to the improvised, all-guns-blazing, 90-second instrumental finale which leads the song to its long fade. Jon Landau, still Springsteen's manager and co-producer, was later heard to describe it as *"The most exciting thing that ever happened in a recording studio."*

Eventually becoming not just the opening track on the album it would lend its name to but the leadoff single as well – along the way providing him with his biggest hit to date – 'Born In The USA' became emblematic on every level of the new path Springsteen was now forced to tread; ironically, not every step of which would meet with his personal approval. An instinctively left-leaning, if typically conservative (with a small 'c'), working-class guy whose personal politics, such as they were, had always resided at basic-survival street-level, Springsteen was appalled to see his anthem of disillusion and regret misinterpreted pretty much across-the-board as an ultra pro-American flag-waver of the first order.

However, as Springsteen was at pains to point out to writer Mark Hagen, the actual story behind the song, 'Born In The USA', was about *"someone returning home (from Vietnam) and trying to find where they belong, if they belong. The music was martial and powerful, expressing a survivor instinct: I have been through this, I am out the other side, and I am alive."*

Nevertheless, the real message of the song was slow to translate to a wider, non-album-buying audience. Released in a US presidential election year, it soon became the victim of political opportunism. Newspaper columnist George Will led the way when he wrote that 'Springsteen is no whiner and the recitation of closed factories and other problems always seemed punctuated by a grand, cheerful affirmation: Born in the USA!' Ouch.

The following summer Clemons, Lofgren, Weinberg, Tallent and Springsteen himself all played on the Jersey Artists For Mankind single organised by Steve Van Zandt, 'Sun City' (with Springsteen also appearing in the subsequent video). Although Springsteen's own long-standing fans were quick to seize upon these actions as all the proof they needed that the Boss had not, counter to appearances, sold out or changed his allegiance, the whole universe of misinterpretation that lay behind 'Born In The USA' continues to haunt the singer to this day. More than 20 million people bought the 'Born In The USA' album, ten times more people than had ever bought any Bruce Springsteen album before or since. For many of those that had come along for the ride on that one album – and would depart again just as quickly by the time of its more low-profile follow-up, 'Tunnel Of Love', three years later – 'Born In The USA' was, quite simply, a song about how good it was to be an American. A decade later, yet another US politician, this time Republican presidential candidate Bob Dole, would again use the song without permission during his 1996 presidential campaign, only for Springsteen's office to intervene yet again, by which time the damage – in terms of perception – had been done. Through it all, however, Springsteen has never wavered from performing the song or having to continually remind large numbers of journalists and politicians about what the song is really all about. As he said in 1999, *"Any work out there is open to different types of interpretation. That is part of the roll of the dice. I probably could have made a record that would have been more easily understood, but... that was the right record."*

In fairness to those that heard but did not listen, 'Born In The USA' was full of deceptively upbeat sounding tracks; moments of apparently warm splendour undercut, on closer inspection, by darker, more wounded reflections. In 'Cover Me', for example, it takes a while to get past the tune which begs to be whistled to hear how much the song's narrator is simply begging for this *"rough old world"* to be firmly shut out of his life. While listening to the other big hit single from the album, 'Dancing In The Dark', with its chirpy synth-line melody and almost childishly catchy chorus swirling about like aural confetti, it's almost impossible to discern without pause to study the lyric sheet just how plaintive and sorrowful the actual song is. The same plus interest can be said for 'Glory Days', its cheesy fairground organ and hell-belting sing-along chorus belying its nervous, booze-sodden message of a man grown old with nothing to offer *"but boring stories"*.

However, there's no mistaking the obvious melancholy of a track as thoughtful as 'Downbound Train', or 'Working On The Highway', where, despite its ritzy upbeat charm, it soon becomes clear that what we have here is actually another bleak prison story. Even the one track explicitly concerned with sweaty, good-for-the-soul sex, 'I'm On Fire', comes with its own guilty-edged atmosphere. It's hard, in fact, to be left in

any doubt as to the album's true assignation once you get to its closing track, 'My Hometown', which Mojo later accurately described as perhaps the most convincing 'conflation of personal and political hard times' in the Springsteen repertoire up to that point, which, the magazine added astutely, 'concludes matters on a note of profound dignity'. For all its outward signs of commercial kowtowing, 'Born In The USA' was 'as much an elegy for America's vanquished soul as 'Nebraska', - exactly so.

After that, the band got into the sessions for the rest of the album like never before, as if making up for the time they personally felt had been lost when their leader had forsaken them for his previous album. So swiftly and intensely did the recording sessions proceed that by the time album was finished Springsteen says he already knew that it was going to be huge. Whether he really knew just how huge, though, is open to conjecture. For when 'Born In The USA' was finally released in June 1984, it became such an enormous international hit – selling more than 20 million copies worldwide and staying afloat in the upper reaches of the world's charts for more than a year – that it would completely transform his life. He may have been a major star since 'Born To Run' in 1975, but now he was truly a global phenomenon, and the ensuing world tour would see him leaving arenas behind to begin headlining huge outdoor football stadiums.

Yet through it all he remained remarkably unfazed, riding his sudden ascent to demigod status as though he had actually seen it all coming.

Not all the critics were easily convinced. Reviewing the Wembley Stadium shows, The Times-critic Richard Williams, a long-standing Bruce supporter, asked outright if 'Born In The USA' was 'not too calculated a simplification of his virtues? Who among his old admirers had not been dismayed by the announcement that his 1985 British tour would consist only of stadium concerts? Could it not be said, in fact, that the past year had been the story of a sell far harder than anything attempted in 1975?' He added scornfully that *"for all but the few hundred crushed closest to the stage there was no feeling of true engagement at all".* He did concede, however, that the second half of the show was infinitely better. *"Where even 'Thunder Road' had sounded coarse and perfunctory, now 'Hungry Heart' and 'Rosalita' shouted their joy to the darkening sky... For the final gallop, ending with 'Twist and Shout', he was joined by his former lieutenant, Steve Van Zandt, whose humorous presence had been missed. Now... the stadium (was) reduced to the dimensions of a club... But – bigger? Louder? Brighter? What happens next?"*

Writing of the show in Newcastle on that tour, Simon Frith of the Observer really hit the nail on the head when he pointed out that *"his live shows have always been the core of the Springsteen myth. The*

Chapter Four

Bruce Springsteen *Glory Days – 50 Years of Dreaming*

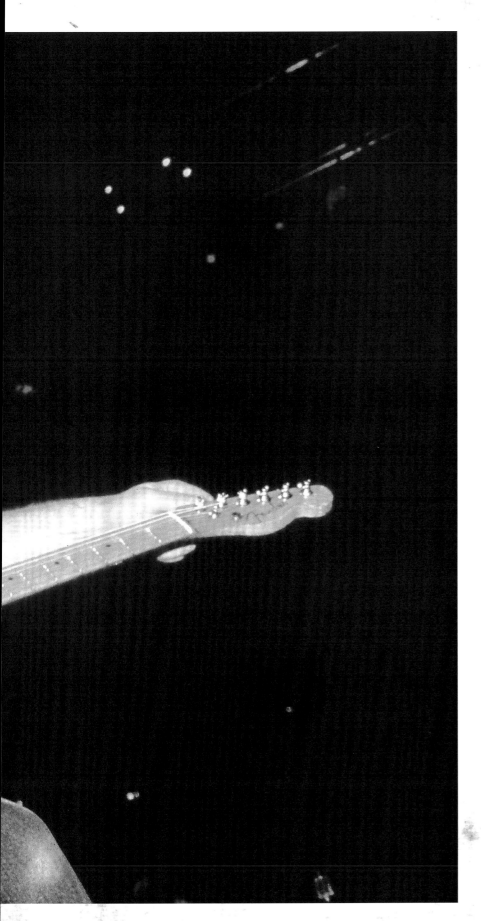

question that's currently being debated then is whether Springsteen's ability to enter his fans' lives can survive his commercially necessary move into stadia and football fields. On the evidence of his opening night in Newcastle on Tuesday, I'd say yes and no — Springsteen can humanise an open-air crowd better than any other rock performer I've seen, but he couldn't completely surmount the distance and discomfort. This clearly worried him. Springsteen needs to feel his audience's response and in Newcastle he worked very hard to get it, eschewing (thank goodness) the alienating device of blowing up video screens, throwing his phenomenal energy into every trick he's ever learnt about crowd control." He concluded: "As he finished his final encore, Springsteen wailed in imitation of James Brown: "I'm just a prisoner, I'm just a prisoner, I'm just a prisoner... of rock and roll!" "

Bizarrely, given that he was now assuming the status of zillionaire rock star, the image 'Born In The USA' saddled Springsteen with was that of the denim-clad blue-collar worker saluting the flag. It wasn't just Bruce who now laboured under this new, somewhat patronising catch-all phrase, but other artisans of the dusty American road like Tom Petty and Bob Seeger. Rock artists that had become stars the hard way: by taking it out on the road; bringing it direct to the 'people' and thereby appearing to have become spokesmen and role models for the ordinary hard-working guy – and his gal. As Springsteen put it to writer Cynthia Rose in 1984, "When I was writing the early songs, the girl was still a part of it, she was just part of the future. But she was always there, that was always there, because it's simply a basic human need. There's a hunger for that relationship. But my characters, they're wrestling with the fact that it's so hard now to separate traditions of love and possession, romance and relationships, from the realities of those things today. It's a puzzle to me, because the desire to become truly involved is as strong as anything about freedom. It's a basic reality of how people are."

Or as Glenn O'Brien wrote in Spin in 1985, "I don't think of Bruce as some flag-waver riding the crest of yuppie reaction. I think of him as the guy who is proving once and for all that you don't have to be an asshole to be an artist. Springsteen is a poet. He writes great words. But he's also a rocker. I listen to some of the older albums and I like them OK. But you live and learn. And if you live and learn right, you get better. I think with 'Nebraska' Bruce really learned how to write and with 'Born In The USA' he really learned how to rock. So I don't care that I just hopped on the bandwagon with the millions. It's just great right now. And I'm happy to be a very avant-garde mainstream far-out regular guy..."

Chapter Four

Chapter Five

If the mind-boggling success of the 'Born In The USA' album and subsequent world tour had been, unquestionably, the pinnacle of Bruce Springsteen's career up to that point, the impressive boxed set that followed, 'Live 1977-1985', summed up and effectively brought to an end a whole era in rock music.

Released in December 1986, just in time for Christmas, on the Monday the album was released in America, absenteeism across the country reached record highs as hundreds of thousands of students and employees called in sick in order to join record shop queues waiting for it to go on sale. Crowds reportedly gathered that sunny day in San Francisco's Golden Gate Park to play the album, while in New Jersey, where the winter weather was much colder, bars unplugged jukeboxes in order to treat their regular patrons to the kind of local 'colour' that didn't come along every day. Excited radio stations across America reported similar scenes, claiming there hadn't been so much genuine, across-the-board interest in a new album's release since The Beatles had unleashed 'Sgt Pepper' on the first day of June in 1967.

Once the initial euphoria had died down, however, what did they find? Well, on first listening, it seemed clear that few if any of the new live recordings actually differed radically from their already familiar versions on the original albums. Indeed, in the case of at least one track, 'No Surrender', many might well argue that the live version was in almost every respect inferior to its recorded original.

Elsewhere, the track listing also drew understandable criticism, comprised as it was of a seemingly disproportionate amount of material from the most recent world tour, thereby forcing fans to essentially buy almost the entire 'Born In The USA' album again. The great saving grace of the live collection, however, was that it underlined what has always been one of the great distinguishing features of the live Bruce Springsteen and the E Street Band experience: that no matter how many times they may have performed the same song over the years they always somehow managed to make it sound as though they really were playing it for the very first time. As ever, spontaneity was the key and there were several examples of

it on 'Live 1977-1985': from the colourfully psychedelic introduction to the rip-roaring 'Cover Me' to the blink-and-you'll-miss-it Elvis Costello impersonations in the sauntering 'I'm On Fire'. Even 'Born In The USA', so familiar on radio and MTV by this point as to be positively nauseating, comes spectacularly alive again in this context, Bruce howling at the song's emotionally shattering climax like a wounded lion. And there were the touchstone classics that no Springsteen live set would now be complete without: a fraught yet tender 'Darkness On The Edge Of Town' suddenly rent asunder by the thunderous sound of Clemons' mighty sax cutting in; Max Weinberg apparently losing all control and actually turning into a monster at the brutal finale to 'Two Hearts'.

Perhaps most affecting, though, was the acoustic section spearheaded by Springsteen's heartfelt rendition of Woody Guthrie's old chestnut 'This Land Is Your Land' and featuring mainly material from the still much-misunderstood 'Nebraska' album. Some may have argued that less pensive acoustic material and more showstoppers of the 'Cadillac Ranch' and 'You Can Look (But You Better Not Touch)' variety would have served the album's purpose better, but that was to miss the point. Hearing the 'Nebraska' songs again, not sung alone this time in a shadowy room but in front of a foot-stomping live audience brought home even more acutely just how important these songs remained to Springsteen, not just as an artist but as a man.

Other major highlights included, for the first time on record (outside of the inevitable bootlegs), Springsteen's own definitive versions of songs he had originally written for other artists, like the shimmering rendition of 'Fire' (originally done for Robert Gordon, though actually the bigger hit for the Pointer Sisters) and 'Because The Night', which proto-punk-poetess Patti Smith had previously enjoyed her biggest hit with as far back as 1979. And of course, no Springsteen/E Street Band show would ever have been complete without a whole swathe of blistering-to-the-touch cover versions of their own, from the full-bodied performance featured here of the Stax classic 'Raise Your Hand' to a passionately over-the-top reading of Edwin Starr's 'War' and a

Chapter Five

tear-jerking, almost too gorgeous-bordering-on-corny version of Tom Waite's surprisingly tender 'Jersey Girl'. For serious aficionados of Springsteen's live output over the years, however, the omission of such long-established stage delights as Manfred Mann's 'Pretty Flamingo' and Gary US Bonds' 'Quarter To Three' was a disappointment. As was the puzzling paucity of in-depth sleeve notes.

Reviewing the boxed set for Creem in March 1987, John Mendelssohn summed up the critical ambivalence towards much of the release when he wrote: *"The 'Born In The USA' tour stuff, all recorded on digital 24-track equipment, is an audiophile's delight... Such ambiance! The sound can get pretty mushy elsewhere, though (especially) in 'Because The Night' and 'Candy's Room'. And the poor Big Man's sax solo on 'Badlands' sounds as though it was recorded from somewhere on the Arizona State University campus. (And) would it have been too much trouble for somebody to have annotated the deluxe booklet that accompanies the album, so that we'd know where and when the many photographs inside were taken, and exactly who's in 'em?"*

It seemed a fair comment, particularly as the rumour preceding the release of the boxed set had spoken of a fully annotated collection of both live material and studio out-takes that was supposed to serve as not just a live album but an actual history of Bruce and the E Street Band taking in virtually every line-up of the band there had ever been, starting, it was said, with a recording from an early gig at My Father's Place club, in Roslyn, New York, in July 1973, when original keyboardist David Sancious and former drummer Vini Lopez were still in the band, as well as several other significant pre-'Miami' Steve Van Zandt moments (including one track featuring the now-obscure Sukie Lahav on violin).

Sadly, for whatever reasons, that project was eventually shelved and replaced by the less ambitious release of 'Live 1977-1985'.

Meanwhile, back home in his new million-dollar mansion in the Palas Verdes area of California (replete with swimming pool, floodlit tennis courts and a helicopter landing pad), by the end of what would become easily the longest, most prestigious, certainly the biggest, dollar-grossing world tour of his career, Springsteen was said to be headed for burn-out on every level – *"Bruced out!"* as he so succinctly put it. It wasn't just the stresses of being on the road for such a long time either. By the time 'Live 1977-1985' was released, he had been off the road for almost a year and had not released any new material for two. Even under those circumstances, though, sometimes it felt like the whole world was leaning over his shoulder, trying to get in on the action. In the weeks that followed the end of the 'Born In The USA'

Bruce Springsteen Glory Days – 50 Years of Dreaming

Chapter Five

Bruce Springsteen *Glory Days - 50 Years of Dreaming*

tour, he reportedly turned down $12 million from Chrysler to appear in a 30-second ad spot with 'Born In The USA' as the musical backdrop. Undeterred, Chrysler met his refusal head-on by shamelessly hiring a Springsteen imitator to sing la Bruce for its cheesily named 'The Pride Is Back' ad campaign.

Adding insult to injury, it was around this time that two of Springsteen's most trusted former senior roadies, Mike Batlin (credited with helping him record – as the tape-op – the home-made album 'Nebraska' in 1982) and Doug Sutphin publicly accused him of refusing to deliver on back-pay and promised 'loyalty' bonuses, in the form of royalties, before firing them for accidentally damaging his canoe. At first, Springsteen denied everything and so the two made good on their promise to sue.

Although Springsteen later shrugged off the episode as *"just one of those things"*, the 1987 lawsuit would eventually take over a year to wend its way through the American courts, by which time the damage to the Boss's reputation had been done. A canoe? It was hardly the image most of his fans had of him; let alone the added mystery of the claim that he, the perceived champion of the working class, actually owed his own employees money?

At such times there was only thing for it, and just as he had in the wake of the intrusive hurly-burly caused by the breakthrough success of 'Born To Run' ten years before, Springsteen retreated from the new-found, massive point-to-point fame afforded him by 'Born In The USA' and, rather than confine himself to coming up with some sort of cash-register-friendly, identikit follow-up, he returned home and began working on a set of entirely different songs; quieter, less rabble-rousing, less outward-looking and observational; more personal and inward-looking than anything he had done since his 'Darkness On The Edge Of Town' days.

The result, released in October 1987, was 'Tunnel Of Love', another ironic title, but one that this time no-one could possibly be left in any doubt about. Another round of critical raves couldn't disguise the surprise most long-term Bruce-watchers felt when they first got to hear 'Tunnel Of Love'. Only the romantic, lyrical 'All That Heaven Will Allow' seemed to shed any light on his, until then, presumed happy marriage. Instead, most of the songs seemed to veer towards a melancholy, sceptical tone that appeared to belie Bruce's newfound success, both personally and professionally. A beautifully weighted, low-key affair, in fact most of the songs, he later confessed, were drawn from the inner emotional turmoil he was going through behind the scenes, for in truth his marriage was actually falling apart. The track 'Two Faces'

Chapter Five

was typical, suggesting a painfully divided soul, desperately reaching out its hands in search of resolution, doing *"things I don't understand"* that ultimately make the singer feel *"like half a man..."*, while plaintive yet touchingly understated new set pieces such as 'Brilliant Disguise' and the bruising 'Tougher Than The Rest', featuring melodramatic synthesizers and a heart-rending harmonica solo at the brittle climax, offered plenty of atmosphere yet little if any of the old gut-punching bluster. Love, it seemed, was no longer the answer, more simply a possibility; the prize only the lucky few truly ever won.

In retrospect, it's easy to view the title track, 'Tunnel Of Love', and the angry, yet curiously emotionally ambivalent-sounding 'All That Heaven Will Allow', as songs that speak directly of the double-edged sword that the massive success of 'Born In The USA' had become. Yet there was also clearly more going on here. Two years short of his 40th birthday, ultimately the singer seemed to be working towards freeing himself of his own two-dimensional image, trying above all else to rediscover a way of expressing himself as an individual, not a star, talking more directly to his audience rather than speaking for them in some greater, far more generalised aspect he had now grown tired, bored and, in truth, horribly frustrated with.

The haunting 'One Step Up' seemed to echo these sentiments, yet nowhere was this feeling more acutely expressed, perhaps, than on the B-side of the 'Tunnel Of Love' single, on the track 'Roulette', a fiercely apocalyptic song about the horrors of nuclear power where he squarely laid the blame at the feet of the political and industrial leaders who *"keep on playing roulette with my life, roulette, with my kids and wife..."*.

The eerily quiet 'Walk Like A Man' seemed to be another from the long line of songs written about his fractured boyhood relationship with his father. Mainly, though, new songs like 'Spare Parts' concentrated on the painful personal experiences of people for whom nothing would ever be so cut and dried again. A raggedy blues excursion that expanded on the familiar but lonely story of a young woman deserted by her fiancé after the ill-timed discovery that she is pregnant, the fact that they are both to blame, both responsible, does nothing to stop the story ending badly, the woman alone, her only option to pawn her once-cherished engagement ring for some *"good cold cash"*.

Despite its low-key profile, the 'Tunnel Of Love' album still went straight to Number 1 in Britain, America and many other countries, though sales fell well below that of both 'Born In The USA' and the 'Live 1977'-1985' boxed set. The inevitable worldwide tour that followed was similarly low-key; no stadiums this time, but back to arenas. Before the tour kicked off in February 1988, however, Bruce took time out to attend the induction of Bob Dylan into the Rock'n'Roll Hall Of Fame, at the plush Waldorf-Astoria Hotel, in New York. Giving a speech before he welcomed Dylan to the stage, Springsteen recalled the first time he ever heard a Bob Dylan record on the radio and how it, quite literally, changed his life. *"I was in the car with my mother and we were listening to, I think, WMCA, and on came that snare shot that sounded like somebody'd kicked open the door to your mind – 'Like A Rolling Stone'. And my mother, she was no stiff with rock'n'roll, she used to like the music, she listened, she sat there for a minute and she looked at me and said, "That guy can't sing". But I knew she was wrong, you know. I sat there and I didn't say nothin', but I knew that I was listening to the toughest voice that I had ever heard. It was lean and it sounded somehow simultaneously young and adult. And I ran out and I bought the single. Then I went out and I got 'Highway 61' and that was all I played for weeks; looked at the cover with Bob in that satin blue jacket and the Triumph motorcycle shirt."*

He concluded by describing Dylan as *"a revolutionary. The way that Elvis freed your body, Bob freed your mind and showed us that just because the music was innately physical did not mean that it was anti-intellect. And he changed the face of rock'n'roll for ever and ever."*

The 'Tunnel Of Love' world tour opened at The Centrum arena in Worcester, Massachusetts, on February 25th, 1988. Out on the road for the first time in two years, the stadiums of the 'Born In The USA' tour had now been cut back on, multiple nights at comparatively more 'intimate' arenas and theatres taking their place. In truth, this may have had as much to do with the fact that, despite reaching the top of the charts, 'Tunnel Of Love' was hardly in the same league when it came down to sheer sales, eventually selling less than half what 'Born In The USA' had done over a similar period. But if Springsteen's audience had shrunk again, shedding the one-off album-buyers and bandwagon-jumpers, it was, his performances seemed to be saying, for the best.

As writer Geoffrey Himes noted in his March 1988 review of the show in The Baltimore Sun, *"if it could be argued that Springsteen had actually avoided making his own left-leaning political beliefs too explicit during the 'Born In The USA' tour, in order to keep his music as accessible to the widest possible audience, on the 'Tunnel Of Love' tour, a rather different, harder-edged Springsteen was no longer trying to be everybody's friend. In Philadelphia, he did a vicious parody of right-wing preachers which included the declaration that "Pat Robertson can't save my soul; in fact, Pat Robertson can kiss my ass!" "*

Chapter Five

There was also a more pointed version of Edwin Starr's 'War', a chestnut of so many previous tours, but here given even more transformative power by allowing Weinberg's thunderous drum finale to segue the song straight into 'Born In The USA'. It was, Himes noted, *"the kind of moment that rock'n'roll was made for... no one would misinterpret 'Born In The USA' as a pro-Rambo anthem this time around."*

Of the new 22-song set, not including the inevitable encores, which could last up to another half hour and comprise as many as six more tunes, there were eight songs from 'Tunnel Of Love', surprisingly just four from 'Born In The USA', and some nights no fewer than six brand new songs, that had never actually featured on any previous Springsteen album, including 'Light Of Day', written for the little-known movie of the same name and originally performed by Joan Jett. Of the other new songs, most memorable was 'I'm A Coward When It Comes To Love', which sounded like it might have been a distant relative of the rollicking 'Pink Cadillac', and the surprisingly reggae-ish 'Part Man Part Monkey', which appeared to deal head-on with the ticklish subject of 'creationism', and in which Springsteen actually bounded about at one point, imitating an ape!

Most tellingly, perhaps, there were just two songs included from his four classic albums in the 1970s. Conspicuous by their absence were such previous goliaths of the Springsteen stage show as 'Backstreets', 'Jungleland' and 'Thunder Road', to name just three. Speaking after the first show, he told journalists back stage, *"I just felt I'd have to drop all the cornerstones of my set. You just can't come out and push people's buttons with old songs. I was interested in personalising my music. You have to re-invent yourself... The only trick to writing a new song is you have to have a new idea. And to have a new idea, you've got to be a bit of a new person."*

Even with the old songs he still played he quite often changed the arrangement so that it sounded at first as though he were playing another completely new song – most evocatively on 'Born To Run', which he performed as a much slower, folksier-sounding song, accompanied only by his own acoustic guitar, and which he repeatedly told audiences was still his own favourite song. *"This is an old song which I wrote when I was 24 years old,"* he was fond of telling audiences, *"sitting on the edge of my bed in Long Branch, New Jersey, and thinking, 'Here I come, world!' When I wrote it, I guess I figured it was a song about a guy and a girl who wanted to run and keep on running. But as I got older and as I sang it over the years, it sort of opened up, and I guess I realised that it was about two people searching for something better. Anyway, this song has kept me good company on my search. I hope it's*

kept you good company on your search." Instead of Clarence Clemmons' honking sax solo at the end there was instead Bruce's own much more plaintive-sounding harmonica, the audience spontaneously providing the familiar 'whoa-whoa-whoa' refrain.

The E Street Band was, as ever, in doubly fine form, though the line-up had been expanded even further for this trip with the addition of the horn section from Southside Johnny's Asbury Jukes outfit, and Patty Scialfa taking a more forward position both vocally and visually than she had ever dared on the 'Born In The USA' tour. The fact that she was also now Bruce's not-so secret girlfriend raised certain eyebrows. Giving the 'old lady' a prominent role in the band contained more than a shade of Linda McCartney sneered certain critics, but Bruce would not be swayed. Patti was a skilled and useful practitioner, he argued, an invaluable addition to the musical texture of the newly expanded group.

Not that Patti's backstage presence, or even the fact that Springsteen was still technically with his wife, Julianne, would stop certain high-profile admirers from trying it on. On April 5th, as Springsteen returned to his dressing room after his second night performing at the Capitol Centres in Andover, Maryland, there was a handwritten note on perfumed paper waiting for him. Written by Fawn Hall, the leggy blonde recently made famous as Lieutenant Colonel Oliver North's document-shredding secretary in the Ronald Reagan-Contragate affair – and subsequently 'close personal friend' of teen-heartthrob actor Rob Lowe. The note read simply: *"I'm Fawn Hall. I'd like to meet you."* With barely a pause for thought, Bruce wrote back: *"I don't like you, I don't like your boss, I don't like what you did. Thank you."*

He received a less controversial though almost as perplexing message after the first of what would be five sold-out nights at Madison Square Garden in New York in May, when famed TV sex therapist Dr. Ruth told him backstage, *"I like what you say about love and sex, but there's one more thing you need to include in your show – contraception."* The Boss's puzzled response: *"Gee, it's gonna be tough to get the word 'contraception' into a song."*

But there were much more serious messages awaiting his attention once the 37-date US leg of the tour ended and the Springsteen entourage flew to London to begin preparing for the UK and European leg of the tour. Although Bruce now knew he was in love with Patti Scialfa, at first they tried hard to keep the relationship a secret. All hell broke loose, though, when the British tabloids eventually broke the story. The first report published in the Sun, on May 26th 1988, carried quotes allegedly from a New York barman who claimed the singer had confessed to him over several beers that he and wife Julianne had split up *"because she wouldn't give him a baby"*. The paper followed that hurtful little revelation up with further 'eye-witness' reports that Springsteen had been on a drunken 'bender' in Los Angeles with U2 singer, Bono, after his latest 'heart to heart' with Julianne.

The real capper came though two weeks later when the same paper, while Springsteen was on tour in Italy, ran an 'exclusive' boasting *"The pictures that will cost The Boss £75 million"* – i.e. Half Springsteen's estimated wealth should his wife divorce him. Taken by long-range telephoto lens, the blurred pix showed Springsteen standing on a Rome hotel balcony with Patti Scialfa, accompanied by others showing him sitting with her on a poolside lounger kissing her. Springsteen declined to comment publicly on the pictures but behind the scenes he was said to be furious.

Meanwhile, back on the road, Bruce used the second of two shows in Stockholm, in July, to announce his participation in the forthcoming Amnesty International Human Rights Now! world tour. His involvement in the Amnesty tour had come about after he was visited backstage after the second of his two-night stint at the Shoreline Amphitheater near Palo Alto, in San Francisco, back in May. Peter Gabriel had flown in personally to persuade Springsteen to sign up for what would be an all-star world tour he had planned in conjunction with Al America's Executive Director, Jack Healey. After chatting to Jon Landau about the idea on the band bus, however, Gabriel left again unsure whether he'd made any real impression. Two weeks later, however, during the five-night stint at Madison Square Garden, Jack Healey himself spent the afternoon going through the practicalities of the proposed tour with Landau and Springsteen's booking agent, Frank Barsalona. Asked to speak to Bruce alone after the show, Healey later described the meeting. *"I go into this long room and there's Bruce, very tired with a terry cloth on him and he just said, "Tell me about human rights". So I blithered on for 50 minutes, giving it my best shot. He just stared the whole time and didn't say a word apart from two questions: one was about American Indians and the other was about refugees. At the end he said, "Well, what can I do?" I swallowed hard and said, "You have to do the whole tour". He just said, "OK, whatever it takes. I'll be there". I was overcome and, being Irish, I leapt on him, hugged him and he started crying."*

In a formal statement he would later make on behalf of the Amnesty tour, Bruce said, *"When you're young and you pick up a guitar, it feels so powerful. It feels like you pulled the sword from the stone. But as you get older you realise that, although it can do a lot of things, there are also a lot of things it can't do. I used to believe that it could save the world, but I don't really believe that any more... As I've got older one of the things I've wanted to do with my music is somehow take that power that I got from those records when I was a kid and somehow put it to work in some nuts-and-bolts way. And I've tried to find out who the people are out there who are working in the trenches, who are taking those ideas and ideals – same ideas and ideals that I got from those records – and putting them to use in some pragmatic way."*

A few weeks after the announcement, during a specially arranged show in East Berlin (billed as the unofficial start of the previously arranged Nicaragua solidarity festival, with all proceeds going to the Karl Marx Hospital in Managua) which was broadcast live on East German radio, Springsteen introduced Dylan's 'Chimes Of Freedom' by saying, in German, *"I am not here today in support of, or opposition to, any government. I'm here to play some rock'n'roll music for East Berliners in the hope that someday all the barriers between us will be torn down."* The second sentence was cut, however, by the ever-watchful old guard establishment figures that ran the station.

The official 'Tunnel Of Love' European tour ended at the start of August. The Amnesty International Human Rights Now! Tour began on September 1st, kicking off in London where the tabloids ran with the unsavoury story of Julianne announcing her decision to divorce her estranged husband after she and Bruce had *"burnt up the telephone lines trying to hash out our future"*. Meanwhile, along with all the other artists on the bill – including Sting, Peter Gabriel and Sinead O'Connor – Springsteen was busy undergoing his first official Amnesty press conference, in lieu of the first official date of the tour at Wembley Stadium. *"Rock'n'roll can offer a transcendent moment of freedom,"* he announced grandly.

But the speech got no further as he found himself buried under an avalanche of questions about the uncertain state of his marriage; questions he steadfastly refused to answer.

Musically, the Amnesty shows saw Springsteen revert to the kind of crowd-pleasing material he had fallen back on during the enormous 'Born In The USA' tour, though via a much more streamlined set: just 15 songs, including the E Street Band backing the entire company on the final song of the night, 'Chimes Of Freedom'. A move which also saw Clarence Clemons returned to centre stage, and Patti Scialfa somewhat conveniently returned to the relative anonymity of the backline chorus. As the tour progressed, the set would also include a duet with Sting on an emotionally charged version of 'The River'.

Bruce Springsteen *Glory Days - 50 Years of Dreaming*

Speaking to the official tour biographer before the show in Barcelona on September 10th, Bruce claimed his band was *"happier than they've been in years, but one of the reasons I wanted to do this was because I wanted to work with other artists. I haven't toured with any other bands since I was 24. I wanted to work in a collective of some sort. I wanted to get in with a bunch of people who had an idea and subsume my identity into that idea, into that collective, and try to come out with something that's more meaningful and bigger and better than I could do on my own."*

In October, as the tour reached Harare, in Zimbabwe, Springsteen was spotted lurking in a record shop buying cassettes of various albums by African artists. Speaking from the stage that night he introduced Edwin Starr's 'War' to the 15,000-strong white South Africans in the crowd with the words: *"There can be no peace without justice and where there is apartheid – systematic as in your country or economic as in mine – there is no justice, there is only war."* Flying into Abidjan on the Ivory Coast the next day, Springsteen elaborated on the theme of his onstage comments the night before.

"Unfortunately," he concluded, *"most of the audiences I draw in the US are white. In Harare I had my first chance to play to an integrated audience. Looking out and seeing black hands raised with white hands was a very emotional moment for me."*

Having flown over 35,000 miles to play to more than an estimated million people, the singer's Amnesty tour drew to a close exactly a week later with a massive sold-out concert in Buenos Aires, Argentina.

Because of unforeseen technical difficulties, what was supposed to be a seven-hour live worldwide radio broadcast ended up including only 100 minutes of music (less than half the length of Springsteen's own usual set) and was disappointingly padded out with banal interviews and high-velocity spot-ads for tour sponsors Reebok and Trojan condoms. Nevertheless, Bruce was moved enough by the tour to tell the final press conference on the eve of the last show how *"this tour was about trying to assert myself as a world citizen. As a boy all I knew of Africa and India and South America was what I studied in geography class. And I wasn't a very good student. The end of this tour marks my graduation of sorts. And I hope that I'll be able to go back home and, in my music, write about a different sensibility that I felt. And I hope to get American young people out of their shell."*

Chapter Five

Chapter Six

The end of the 1980s found Bruce Springsteen exposed in ways that would have been unimaginable at the start of the decade. On the positive side, his involvement in the Amnesty Human Rights Now! tour had deepened the greatly expanded political awareness that had begun with his introduction to the reading lists and ideas of his manager and mentor, Jon Landau. The downside was that his personal life had never been under such public scrutiny before.

There was the 'scandal' of his broken marriage to Julianne Phillips and his increasingly public affair with Patti Scialfa; and there was the perplexing business of the lawsuit he was having to contest with his disgruntled former roadies.

Under the circumstances, it would have been understandable if Springsteen had completely dropped out of sight at this point, as had been his custom anyway at the end of previous long tour cycles.

Curiously, however, he chose to maintain a fairly public persona throughout the last months of the '80s.

In November 1988, on a visit to spend the Thanksgiving holidays with his parents in San Francisco, he stopped off in the early hours at the Stone Club where he jumped up onstage with his old pals, Southside Johnny & the Asbury Jukes, themselves now permanently resident out on the West Coast, where they belted through high-spirited versions of 'In The Midnight Hour', 'Little Queenie' and several others.

A few weeks later, with the first stage of his divorce now completed and the decree absolute to follow in March, Bruce and Patti, now living together, prepared to spend their first official Christmas together in LA. Film and music impresario Robert Stigwood was said to have offered him £10 million to play Che Guevara, opposite Meryl Streep in the title role, in a projected movie version of Tim Rice and Andrew Lloyd Webber's hit stage musical, Evita. An offer Springsteen declined without a second thought.

New Year 1989, meanwhile, found the singer ensconced in a Los Angeles studio, where he was whispered to be working on a Patti Scialfa solo album, while at the same time also recording demos for his own next project. Later that month, he made his now-regular appearance at the annual Rock'n'Roll Hall Of Fame show, where he sang a heart-rending version of 'Crying'

in tribute to his old hero, Roy Orbison, who had sadly died just before Christmas. He ended this brief performance on an up note though, jamming with Mick Jagger and Keith Richards, plus Patti, original E Street Band drummer Vini Lopez, and George Theiss.

In March, the 'canoe case' finally came to court in New Jersey, the judge throwing out Batlin and Sutphin's damages claims for 'emotional distress' but allowing that their case for unpaid overtime had grounds to proceed. Unabashed, a week later Springsteen attended an early evening party in LA for former world champion boxer Ray 'Boom Boom' Mancini, before moving on to Rubber, a new club owned by Hollywood heartthrob Mickey Rourke. Needing no encouragement to jump up and jam with local bar band the Mighty Hornets, Bruce blasted out 'CC Rider' with them. In the days that followed, US and British tabloids reported on the impending marriage of Bruce and Patti, with Rourke as their best man. The next few months passed in relative silence, however, and whatever plans Bruce and his new lover may have had were kept strictly private.

The summer of 1989 saw a flurry of further Springsteen activity as the singer embarked on a series of impromptu appearances that would belatedly become christened The Summer Club Tour '89. It began in June, when Springsteen agreed to make a low-key guest appearance at old haunt the Stone Pony club in New Jersey with drummer Max Weinberg's jazz-jive big band, Killer Joe – also assisted by Patti and E Street keyboardist Roy Bittan – in support of the annual Jersey Shore Jazz & Blues Festival.

Part of a more concerted effort to revive the local music scene, Springsteen was aghast to learn that the Asbury Park Rock'n'Roll Museum and Palace Amusements, home of the original Tunnel Of Love, had recently been forced to close and that the Pony was also under serious threat of 'municipal redevelopment'.

For the next three months, Springsteen performed at a number of such low-profile events, turning in unannounced guest appearances on no less than 20 different occasions – including jams with Nils Lofgren's band at the Stone Pony, Neil Young on Long Island, Jackson Browne in an Atlantic City casino, Ringo's All Starr Band at the Garden State Arts Centre at Holmdel (the town where he recorded 'Nebraska' in a day) and Gary 'US' Bonds back

Chapter Six

at the Pony. After years spent as virtually a recluse between albums, he now demonstrated a new sociability that apparently included plenty of beer drinking interspersed with the occasional 'kamikaze' vodka cocktail.

In the middle of all this good-time energy, Springsteen also managed to find time to record 'Viva Las Vegas' for 'The Last Temptation Of Elvis', a Nordoff-Robbins Music Therapy benefit album, at One On One Studio, in North Hollywood. His backing band on the session was equally impromptu and featured former Faces and Rolling Stones keyboardist Ian McLagan, plus session superstars, bassist Bob Glaub and drummer Jeff Porcaro.

Perhaps the most significant date in the diary, though, that long hot summer occurred right at its end, on September 23rd, back in New Jersey once again, when a suitably 'refreshed' Bruce celebrated his 40th birthday on the Shore at McCloone's Rumrunner club, in Seabright, with the E Street Band in full attendance, augmented on this special occasion by the one-off return of Steve Van Zandt. Bruce had also flown in his parents from San Francisco and at one point he pulled his mother onstage with him for a dance. His Uncle Warren also featured onstage that night, on backing vocals. As the band rolled into rambunctious versions of 'Twist And Shout' followed by 'Glory Days', Springsteen yelled through the mike: "*I dedicate this song to me! I may be 40 years old but, damn it, I'm still handsome!*" It was such a fun occasion, and Bruce seemed so happy to have everybody there, nobody could possibly have guessed that it was in fact going to be the last time Bruce would appear in public with the E Street Band for another ten years.

The first the band themselves heard of it was just a month later, when Bruce sat down to phone all of them personally, one at a time, beginning with Clarence Clemons, who was on tour in Japan with Ringo's All Starr Band at the time. The sax giant, who had also been through a painful separation from his wife that year, and was one of Bruce's oldest friends as well as being a stalwart of the band right from the first album, took the news particularly hard. "*Everything that I loved,*" he later recalled, "*my family and my music, I lost both of them in the same year, 1989. That was a tough, tough year.*" The phone call from Bruce had "*made me go from being very shocked, to being angry to happy, all in about ten seconds*". On reflection, he said, there was also a sense of relief. Since Patti had arrived on the scene, his role in the E Street Band, both onstage and in the studio, had been diminished. "*I wasn't playing what I wanted to hear. My diminishing role in his music had me crazy. He was getting away from that sound, from the saxophone.*"

The rest of the band was equally shocked. Shocked and, in some cases, bitterly hurt. Even the reported $2 million pay-offs they each received could not sufficiently heal all the wounds. Indeed, despite the fact that they all left as millionaires – the 'Born In The USA' world tour reportedly yielded each member of the E Street Band a cool $4 million alone – they still felt like their world had collapsed.

There had been some suggestion, initially, that the band might pursue an independent recording career on its own, but as Max Weinberg said, "*We were put together strictly to serve Bruce.*" If Bruce didn't need them anymore then the E Street Band would simply cease to be. And that's the way it would stay, it seemed. Perhaps sensing the winds of change in the air, the band had already begun to branch out, in fact, into other areas long before Bruce was to make his fateful decision. 'Miami' Steve had been the first high-profile member to bail out, of course, after the recording of 'Born In The USA', and his replacement, Nils Lofgren, already had a long and distinguished career as a solo artist – and backing musician for Neil Young; now he simply resumed his stalled solo career. Soon the others began to follow suit. Weinberg had played on legendary promoter Bill Graham's Amnesty International fundraising tour in the mid-'80s, and recorded with John Eddie and Miguel Rios; he also had his part-time jazz band; he also took a communications degree and led the house band on Conor O'Brien's TV talkshow.

Clemons had worked on an Aretha Franklin TV special and toured with Ringo Starr; he now resumed session work and formed his own band, The Red Bank Rockers. Danny Federici had already written and recorded as a solo artist; he now built and ran his own studio in Colt's Neck, New Jersey.

Gary Tallent moved to Nashville to play with and produce country and rockabilly bands. Meanwhile, Roy Bittan, who had always kept his hand in as a session player (most famously on David Bowie's 'Station To Station' album) also bought his own studio, in Los Angeles, though he would later be invited back – on a session basis – by Springsteen to play on his 'Human Touch' and 'Lucky Town' albums.

For his part, Springsteen later tried to explain his actions by claiming he had become deeply depressed with what he now saw as the whole "*macho thing*" of having the band – his gang – around him, and the "*iconic role*" that forced him to adopt. He also allowed that his divorce had brought on a deep depression, not at his decision to pull away or that he had fallen in love with someone new, but that his marriage had "*failed*". For the next year, he later confessed, he underwent a long dark night of the soul, making "*life generally unpleasant*" for his new love, Patti, tormenting himself with self-loathing and guilt. "*I spun off for a while*", he shrugged. "*I just got lost… I was in a lot of fear.*" At one point he sought therapy to try and ease his pain and feels he definitely gained some insight into whatever it was that was really ailing him. As Nils Lofgren put it, "*Right now Bruce is just a little… he's searching. He's allowed to be confused.*"

Chapter Six

Bruce Springsteen *Glory Days - 50 Years of Dreaming*

With news of the E Street Band's break-up now official, there was happier news on the home front in January 1990, when it was officially announced that Patti was pregnant with the couple's first child.

Bruce was said to be *"overjoyed"*. He certainly seemed to have a newfound air of relaxation about him when he faithfully turned out for that year's Rock'n'Roll Hall Of Fame bash in Los Angeles. With his hair having grown so long he now tied it back in a ponytail, Bruce and Patti shared a table at the star-studded awards ceremony with Sting. Later that evening, Bruce got up and played along with former Creedence Clearwater Revival leader John Fogerty, before leading the assembled all-star cast in a long and unwieldy 'Long Tall Sally'.

The following month found Springsteen back working hard in LA's Studio City with session superstars, drummer Steve Jordan and bass player Randy Jackson. Inspired by this new musical setting, Springsteen eventually reeled off no less than 15 new numbers, notably one called 'Just Another Roll Of The Dice'. Steve Van Zandt was also to be seen hanging out with his old Boss in the studio. Apart from occasional sightings in public – notably a February appearance in aid of Sting's rainforest charity, accompanied on stage by Paul Simon, Don Henley and Jackson Browne, and in March at a Tom Petty show at the Inglewood Forum, where he jammed with Petty and Bob Dylan on 'Rainy Day Women', and again in April at a special showing of the movie Born On The Fourth Of July, along with Ron Kovic and Tom Cruise – Springsteen would spend the rest of his time that year getting ready for the arrival of his first child, plans for which included the purchase of a new £10 million estate in LA that reportedly included two large houses, a virtual forest of tall eucalyptus trees, but this time no swimming pool or even a tennis court.

With the baby, a boy that the deliriously happy couple named Evan James, born in August, the only other news of note that summer was that a judge had now, thankfully, ruled that Springsteen's tax records were not to be placed in the public domain as had been requested by the lawyers representing Batlin and Sutphin, who now claimed that, in addition to the unpaid overtime they were also victims of a broken promise to have their pay kept just behind the musicians. In retaliation, Springsteen's lawyers claimed the two were paid $225,000 in an ex-gratia severance payment when they left his employ in 1985. It seemed like the case would never go away. In June, meanwhile, Bruce unexpectedly gave his permission for hardcore rap stars 2 Live Crew to sample 'Born In The USA' for their controversial single 'Banned In The USA', in protest at the way they were being censored by parents' pressure groups like the PMRC.

The year ended with a surprise appearance at the Christic Institute benefit – an important independent watchdog on American government

– held at the Shrine Auditorium, in Los Angeles, on November 17th – Springsteen's first proper gig for nearly 20 years without the cushion of the E Street Band to fall back on. He seemed more talkative and relaxed onstage than since his earliest days, becoming positively confessional at different moments. During his introduction to 'My Hometown', for example, he talked about the thrill – and the fear – of becoming a father for the first time. *"The thing of having a baby, you know, you're waiting and you're waiting. Call the doctor. He says, "Wait, wait, don't come down here." So we're waiting. We rented some movies, walked around Beverly Hills for a while.*

Finally, we go to the hospital and I'm thinking, "Okay, I don't wanna faint." That's my main concern. That's disgusting, isn't it? Anyway, we get there and it's night, and it was nice and the baby came pretty quick. Took him home and it was amazing, because I seen the first time he cried, and I caught his first tear on the tip of my finger. Seen his first smile and cleaned his first shit. All those things I think you keep on doing, I guess. Tremors, we watched (the movie) Tremors, to spiritually prepare us for the occasion."

Then when he introduced 'My Father's House' he told another story: *"I had this habit for a long time. I used to get in my car and I would drive back through my old neighbourhood... past the old houses I used to live in... I got so I would do it really regularly, two or three, four times a week, for years, and I eventually got to wondering, what the hell am I doing? So I went to see a psychiatrist, this is true, and I said, "Doc, what am I doing?" So he says, "Well, something bad happened and you keep going back to see if you can fix it or somehow make it right." And I sat there and I said, "That is what I'm doing." And he said, "You can't." "*

Finally, introducing an old but unrecorded song called 'The Wish', he said: *"I wrote this song quite a while ago. I never really recorded it. It's a song about my mother. It was a funny thing because I had this song and I said, "Gee, in rock music, in rock'n'roll, ain't nobody sings about their mother out there."*

It's against all that macho posturing you have to do and stuff. I wanted to figure it out, so I went to see this psychiatrist. And I told him what the problem was. So he said he understood: "You have to see all men are afraid of their mothers. They say a boy's best friend is his mother, but really all men are afraid of their mothers." I had to pay for this, you're gonna get it for free. So I said, "Well, men are afraid of their mothers, yeah." That's why, when a man and woman get arguing, the woman's always going, "Do I look like your mother? I'm not your mother. Am I supposed to be your mother?" Men are always going, "Stop mothering me. Ah, my mother used to do that." So realising the truth of this thing, I said, "Wait a minute. I'm man enough to sing about my mother. I think." So Mom, if you're out there, this better be good...".

Chapter Seven

In terms of his progress as a songwriter, neither Bruce Springsteen's newfound domestic bliss – he and Patti had married in a private ceremony just before the birth of their first child – nor his unexpected decision to break up the E Street Band, appeared to actually further his cause in the early 1990s. For once, in fact, whatever was going on in his personal and/or professional life seemed to have little if any salutary effect on the songs he would now sit down to write. Indeed, it would be almost five years after the release of the subdued 'Tunnel Of Love' before he would release his next work. And then when he did, the first post-E Street albums he produced – the bizarrely simultaneously released 'Lucky Town, and 'Human Touch', in March 1992 – were and remain the most critically reviled of his entire career.

It's not that either album was really dreadful – some of the best moments like 'Better Days', '57 Channels (And Nothin' On)', or the memorable title track to 'Human Touch', all of which, perhaps tellingly, were released as singles – more that neither of the albums was that great. Certainly not by conventional Bruce Springsteen album standards. The complete lack of the familiar E Street wall-of-sound also didn't help; the fact that Springsteen seemed to have chosen to release the band from their duties just as he was writing his most anonymous-sounding material only underlining the feeling amongst certain fans and critics that maybe the Boss had lost his way in the fog of connubial bliss that accompanied his newfound family life. Even highlights like 'Roll Of The Dice', whose genesis went back to before his children (of which he now had two) were born but seemed to be about the joys – and doubts – of fatherhood, or the easy-going 'Living Proof' couldn't dispel the impression that the Boss's new songs lacked a certain cutting edge.

Undeterred by the lukewarm critical reaction, Springsteen announced his first world tour for four years. As usual the shows were all long – in excess of three hours, no support act, just an intermission in the middle. But again, without the flash and thunder of the E Street Band there to add life to proceedings, it seemed like a strangely subdued Springsteen that arrived on stage each night, the honking, luscious sound of the Big Man's saxophone replaced by the weedy synthesizer sound that had become evermore ubiquitous since 'Born In The USA'. Possibly because of the so-so critical reaction the new albums and shows were receiving, by the time the tour reached the UK that summer, Springsteen was refusing all interview requests in favour of hosting what amounted to mini-press conferences to a handful of carefully selected journalists before each show. Reporting on one such occasion for Vox magazine, writer Adam Sweeting led the way by asking how the public at large had reacted so far to the lack of the E Street Band?

Springsteen did his best to reply truthfully: "There was a big banner in Spain that said "Where Is The E Street Band?", So you have to salute the kids, and say, hey, that's a good question! But I believe that the press has been very good so far in other countries, and people have been very flexible with the whole thing." The singer went on to suggest that the live show was less about the gang mentality of old and more to do with the family life that had superseded it. "My relationship with Patti and the children brought an enormous amount of faith and hope. There's little babies! You can't afford despair, you gotta find faith someplace."

No longer the romantic storyteller of 'Born To Run', nor the embittered war-vet of 'Born In The USA', but a happy family man, as he said, "I try to do a lot of things during the course of the night. I try to tell the story I've been in the process of telling for a long time, and then I also try to give people their money's worth and let 'em hear the songs they wanna hear. I'm trying to find an audience that is interested in that story. It's just a human story." Family man or not, onstage he still kept up the banter with the audience, still liked to drop in the occasional topical aside as he introduced his songs from the stage. For example, appearing at the Syracuse Carrier Dome, in New York, in November 1992, he prefaced 'If I Should Fall Behind' with a little speech inspired by the recent victory by the Democrat party in the US presidential elections. "This is for Bill Clinton", he said with a smile. "Back in '85, I used to say, "Nobody wins till everybody wins." But that's not true. There's people out there winning but a lot of others are losing real big. The election is over and this is for Bill... gotta wish him the best."

Giving the induction speech that welcomed another of his former boyhood heroes, Creedence Clearwater Revival, into the Rock'n'Roll Hall

Chapter Seven

Bruce Springsteen *Glory Days - 50 Years of Dreaming*

of Fame, in January 1993, he reminisced about his more idealistic teenage years. "*In 1970*", he began, "*suburban New Jersey was still filled with the kind of '60s spirit (the movie) Easy Rider made us all so fond of. I'm referring to the scene where Dennis Hopper gets blown off his motorcycle by some redneck with a shotgun! A weekend outing at the time was still filled with the drama of possibly getting your ass kicked by a total stranger who disagreed with your fashion sense.*" He went on: "*Into New Jersey came the music of (Creedence Clearwater Revival) and for three minutes and seven seconds of 'Proud Mary' a very strained brotherhood would actually fill the room. It was simply a great song that everybody liked and it literally saved our asses on many occasions.*" Jon Fogerty, he concluded, "*was an Old Testament, shaggy-haired prophet, a fatalist – funny too. He was severe, he was precise, he said what he had to say and he got out of there. He was lyrically spare and beautiful. He created a world of childhood memory and of men and women with their backs to the wall. A landscape of swamps, bayous, endless rivers, gypsy women, back porches, hang-dogs chasing ghosts, devils, bad moons rising, straight out of the blues tradition.*" Something, he seemed to be saying, he now wanted to do himself. Only time would tell if he would be able to pull it off but for now the jury was still out.

Not even the release of the 'MTV Unplugged' album in April 1993 could convince the critics that what we were seeing wasn't a Springsteen in some sort of steady artistic decline. As the eminent British writer, David Sinclair, noted in a June 1993 review for Rolling Stone, "*The creeping realisation that there is more to life than music has quite naturally chipped away at the margins of what Springsteen is now prepared to give – and indeed is capable of giving – in performance.*" He went on: "*Springsteen maintained an impressive energy level, jumping into the crowd during 'Leap Of Faith', flinging himself bodily onto (Roy) Brittan's keyboard during 'Light Of Day' (a pulverising rocker, now available for the first time on the Europe-only release 'MTV Plugged') and hauling up a blonde accomplice from the audience to dance with him during 'Working On The Highway'. But throughout the show we saw more of Bruce the hard-working huckster than Bruce the lion-hearted defender of the true rock'n'roll faith. There were no between-song raps about fatherhood, the state of the nation or the precious things in life. There was, however, the corny business of a dozen or so big furry dice planted in the crowd and flung out onstage at the start of 'Roll Of The Dice'; and there was a questionable version of 'Rockin' All Over The World' that echoed the raucous arena-rock thump of Status Quo's version more closely than John Fogerty's rootsy original.*" He concluded: "*There were moments recalling the greatness of old (but) the bulk of this gig was business as usual.*"

It hardly added up to a ringing endorsement, but Sinclair's views were hardly untypical of the reactions Springsteen's new artistic guise was now attracting, something the perfunctory release of a 'Greatest Hits' album in February 1995 did little if anything to dispel – despite the fact that Springsteen actually reassembled the E Street Band to record a couple of new tracks for inclusion on it: 'This Hard Land' and 'Secret Garden'.

Clarence Clemons had been working on his own album in LA, the instrumental 'Peacemaker', when he got the unexpected call. As he later recalled in Mojo, "*I was planning my birthday party and I got a call, "Come on down, we're gonna play some music." I was pretty shocked. And I went down and I spent my birthday, January 11th, standing in front of a microphone playing saxophone with the E Street Band – the best birthday present I could have had.*" He went on to say that since the band had broken up he felt there had definitely "*been a void*" on his former employer's albums. "*Something's been missing in music for me.*"

Had it been awkward working together again after so long, though? "*No*", he replied, "*it was like yesterday... The joy of seeing everyone together overwhelmed anything else that could have been felt. We recorded a bunch of songs in about three days, and out of the bunch he chose two for the album.*"

If anything, though, the inclusion of the two new E Street-backed tracks only made the critics yearn even more for the 'good old days'. The only respite during this less than satisfactory period occurred in 1994, when Springsteen supplied the demi-title song to the hit movie, Philadelphia, which concerns a lawyer dying of AIDS, played by Tom Hanks, and for which Springsteen composed the moving 'Streets Of Philadelphia' – a fact born out by its enormous success, providing Bruce with not only his biggest hit single since his cluster of hits from the 'Born In The USA' album a decade before, but an Oscar for Best Original Song In A Movie.

But if his musical career was now only moving in fits and starts, on a personal level the first half of the 1990s found Springsteen happier and more fulfilled than he had ever been before. With another child on the way, life with Patti was good. As he said, "*She has a very sure eye for all of my bullshit!*"

He also discovered his own "*terrifying*" capacity to love the three children she bore him during this period. And by 1995, he was ready to dip his toes in the water again by making his most earnest – certainly his most 'downsized' – musical statement since 'Nebraska': the extremely low-key, all-acoustic 'The Ghost Of Tom Joad', released to overwhelmingly enthusiastic critical plaudits in November that year.

This was Bruce Springsteen back to what he does best, strumming simple yet bone-shaking tunes about the poor and disenfranchised, the lost and lonely left behind by the runaway American dream he had once espoused so wholeheartedly in song. Not so much angry as worldly, the clenched fist replaced by the knowing, weary smile, he spun strange, haunting tales of life-after-Vietnam and Watergate, of prisoners – the ones locked up in jails and the ones locked-up in lives of broken dreams and lost loves. Indeed, the chief inspiration behind the new songs, he later explained, had come while he sat at home in his Beverly Hills mansion, taking in the reports on the TV news of the wave upon wave of Mexican and South American immigrants that routinely poured across the border into the US.

Many were caught by border patrols and sent back to the badlands they had desperately sought to escape, while the ones that got through, in search of new, more prosperous lives, often found themselves unemployed, sleeping in cars and walking the hot, mean streets of the LA ghettos. Once again, Springsteen found himself returning to the books of John Steinbeck and the songs of Woody Guthrie, whose themes he was disturbed to find still very much alive in modern-day California. Even the totemic title figure of the new album – Tom Joad – was taken from Steinbeck's dustbowl-era anti-hero from his masterpiece, The Grapes Of Wrath, allowing Springsteen to shed his own personal problems in favour of writing about the more deeply troubled lives of people he had never met yet strongly identified with.

However, unlike the emotionally windswept characters in 'Nebraska' (the only other Springsteen album it resembles), the characters that populate the songs of 'The Ghost Of Tom Joad' have no apparent escape route, consigned to an intrinsically modern hell of rank unemployment, drug addiction, prostitution, prejudice and early deaths. As Springsteen croons on the ghostly title track which opens the album, 'The highway is alive tonight, but nobody's kidding nobody about where it goes...' A theme he returns to with a vengeance on the haunting 'Highway 29', where only capture and death lurk in the dark, forbidding shadows of the roadside for the forlorn figures who return after a bank robbery that goes horribly wrong. No longer born to run, not even born in the USA, this is a world, Springsteen seems to be saying, where none of the old ways work, none of the comforts or joys or even simple sorrows still retain meaning. This, quite simply, is a modern-day version of hell, positioned in the very heart of the Californian dream which he, as the narrow-eyed narrator, finds himself living uncomfortably close by. A netherworld no affluent white man can truly know about, where the broken dreams of the factory worker in 'Straight Time' is simply left waiting to return to a life of crime, lying in bed gazing at the cracked ceiling, 'drifting off into foreign lands'. Or the poor immigrant forced into a life of crime in 'The New Timer' lurks in darkness 'machete by my side' with only 'the name of who I ought to kill' buzzing round his darkened mind. Or, most stark and disturbing of all, perhaps,

the tale of the 'Sinaloa Cowboys' – his grim depiction of border-outlaw Mexicans getting by on methamphetamine and fear, a portrait drawn straight from a disturbing recent article he had read in the Los Angeles Times.

In keeping with his latest musical incarnation, the live shows that followed were equally stark and stripped back. Turning his back on the arenas and stadiums that had sustained him for the previous 20 years, he returned to playing theatres, on his own this time, just him, a microphone, a harmonica and an acoustic guitar to keep him company – allowing the Boss to put on his most affecting and intimate performances since his very earliest days in the bars and clubs of New Jersey. He still sang 'Born In The USA' but more in the spirit of the original, ragged demo, completely omitting the charged-up chorus which, back in 1984, had seemingly made the whole world punch the air. Also conspicuous by its absence from the song was the line about 'the Yellow Man'. This, he seemed to be saying, is what me and that song have always really been about: the little guy standing alone, facing the oncoming crowd naked.

Reporting on Springsteen's new show at the Wiltern Theatre, in Los Angeles, in the January 1996 issue of Mojo, Dave Di Martino wrote how Bruce, *"now an Angelino of some duration, had just advised potential BRROOOCE screamers that his forthcoming songs needed to be listened to by an attentive, quiet audience"*. He went on: *"Few can fault Springsteen for his sense of pacing; indeed, most of the new songs were delivered between stripped-down versions of more familiar ones. Along with second number, 'Adam Raised A Cain', a total of nine older tracks were acoustically reworked, some of them drastically... the older songs Springsteen chose to sing – 'Nebraska' and 'Darkness On The Edge Of Town', say – were a perfect thematic fit with his newer work. That theme in full: life sucks and then you die. A far cry from the joyful tinge of his recent work – but then again, 'Living Proof' and '57 Channels' seemed drawn from what appears to be his own very happy personal life. 'The Ghost Of Tom Joad', on the other hand, seems drawn from books, articles and films – several of which are courteously listed on the album's liner notes for your perusal."*

Or as Phil Sutcliffe pointed out in a later issue of the same magazine, *"Until Bruce Springsteen took to the road as an acoustic folkie singing about poverty, drugs and human dereliction with the songs from 'The Ghost Of Tom Joad' in 1995, many critics clove to the notion that he was just the grease-monkey bard of cars-and-girls culture. But this was only because they didn't listen and missed nearly everything."*

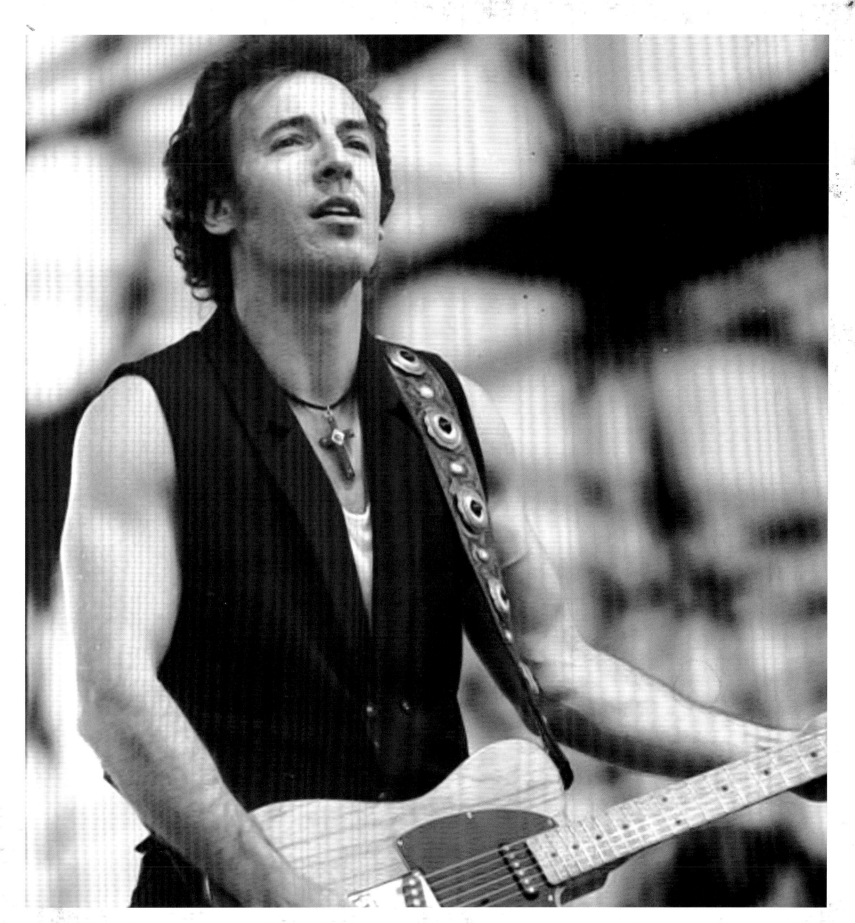

Chapter Seven

Chapter Eight

Despite the stunning return to form marked by the release of 'The Ghost Of Tom Joad', Bruce Springsteen has only released two more albums of all-original material in the 11 years since its climactic release – though, arguably, they were both worth the wait as each was received with the kind of wide-eyed rapture from both fans and critics alike that used to be reserved for almost everything he did back in the 1970s and '80s. A period punctuated by a series of live and compilation packages – some welcome like the 'Tracks' boxed set in 1998, a worthy addition to the canon, including as it did an interesting array of previously unreleased tracks, most notably the original 'Nebraska'-era acoustic version of 'Born In The USA', as was the excellent 'Live In New York City' in 2001; some less so, like the decidedly non-essential gap-filler 'The Essential Bruce Springsteen' collection in 2003 – perhaps the biggest testament to the power of Springsteen's enduring appeal is that his hardcore audience has hardly diminished, nor indeed his consistently high standing in the critical community.

Most welcome was his decision to put back together the fabled E Street Band, including the return of Steve Van Zandt on guitar. Originally reacquainted in the studio for the two extra tracks on the 1995 'Greatest Hits' compilation, Springsteen had finally given in to public pressure and reinstated the band as his live backing outfit with their first fully-fledged tour together in nearly 15 years in 2000 – a reunion road trip that culminated at Madison Square Garden, with the final show of the tour being filmed and recorded for the 'Live In New York City' CD, DVD and HBO special which followed. As Clarence Clemons had said in an earlier, 1995 Mojo interview, *"The E Street Band cut its own niche in rock'n'roll and made its own space, and although this space was filled with another band, it wasn't really filled. What the E Street Band did with Bruce was something that was very strong and could never be replaced."* He also pointed out that they had stayed in touch during the years when they weren't working together. *"We'd talk every now and then… He's my son's godfather. It's kind of like family. It's like being married to someone. Whenever we do play together you look at each other thinking, this is the way it's supposed to be…"*

Needless to say, the world tour was rapturously received, as was a new song performed by the band, 'American Skin' – a scathing indictment on the alleged shooting by NYPD officers of an unarmed Bronx resident named Amadou Diallou. This so incensed the New York police force, however, that spokesmen actually called for Springsteen and the E Street Band's shows at Madison Square Garden that year to be boycotted.

With the sting apparently back in the tail of the Boss's new songs, 'The Rising', his first studio album back with Clemons and co. released in 2002, was eagerly anticipated. On the surface, a moving response to the terrorist atrocities of 9/11 that resulted in the loss of more than 3,000 lives in New York, Washington and Pennsylvania, most notably the traumatised-sounding 'Nothing Man', written from the perspective of the ordinary working people whose lives had been irreparably damaged or disfigured beyond recognition by the calamitous attacks spearheaded by the destruction of the Twin Towers.

Tracks like 'Further On (Up The Road)' also exemplified the charged mood of the album: an ominous beat burnished by menacing massed guitars, a song in the tradition of 'Thunder Road' or 'Adam Raised A Cain', though less verbose, its direct, almost spoken lyrics stripped of verbosity, the message straight to the point. 'Empty Sky', another powerful stand-out moment featuring a wonderfully distinctive melody and driving, evocative verses, was almost too painfully direct, its chorus depicting the singer looking out at a very different New York skyline the day after the attacks: 'Empty sky/ Empty sky/ I woke up this morning to an empty sky', the message being driven home even deeper by the emotional background vocals from wife Patti. Other highlights included the equally challenging 'Into The Fire', the melancholy 'Paradise', the all-too-painful 'You're Missing', and 'My City Of Ruins', a song actually written sometime before about the slow degradation of his own home town, Asbury Park, but re-forged here as an every-song for the crumbling ruins of New York – all this with Springsteen singing throughout probably better, certainly more movingly, than at any point previously in his career. There was also a special version of the album in hardback, mock-book form, along with a batch of extra photos and handwritten notes from the Boss himself. As a result, it would eventually earn Springsteen no less than three Grammy awards – including the much-coveted Album Of The Year prize – for the courageous and outspoken views of its hard-hitting lyrics.

The new album also found him back on the cover of Time magazine again – 27 years after his first controversial appearance as 'Rock's New Sensation'. The headline this time: *"Reborn In The USA: How Bruce Springsteen reached out to 9/11 survivors and turned America's anguish into art."* In the ensuing article, Springsteen revealed how the initial inspiration for the new 14-track album had come when, a few days after the September 11th atrocities, he was leaving a parking lot in the Jersey Shore town of Sea Bright, when a fan rolled down his car window and shouted toward him, *"We need you!"* Speaking to the New York Times a few weeks before its release, Springsteen also revealed how the shock of 9/11 had actually brought him out of a prolonged writer's block and allowed him to find his *"rock voice"* again.

Not quite everyone, though, got the same deep feeling from listening to the album. American writer Michael Goldberg was particularly scathing. *"He may be on the cover of Time again, but 'The Rising' sure ain't 'Born To Run' "*, he wrote, going on to describe what he admitted was one of the best tracks on the album, 'Let's Be Friends (Skin To Skin)' as 'almost a throwaway'. Then adding insult to injury by proclaiming: *"If only the rest of 'The Rising' were as good... it's been a long time since Springsteen made a really good album of new material. You have to reach back to 1987 and 'Tunnel Of Love'..."*

Released at the end of July 2002, 'The Rising' also received a panning review in Newsweek – though some argued that was the inevitable price to be paid for offering an exclusive interview to its main rival Time first, who had, in contrast, described 'The Rising' as 'the first significant piece of pop art to respond to the events of that day'. Rave reviews also followed in quick succession from influential sources like the Wall Street Journal, Rolling Stone and Mojo – reactions more typical of the general critical response. The public response was no less ecstatic, resulting in 'The Rising' rocketing straight to Number 1 in the US, where it had sold more than half a million copies in its first week of release alone – the biggest first-week sales of any Springsteen album in over a decade. Even more impressive, 'The Rising' would also debut at Number 1 in ten other countries, including Britain, Canada, Germany, Spain and Sweden. (In an interesting footnote, the huge success of 'The Rising' had the knock-on effect of replacing another, though quite different 9/11-inspired album at the top of the US charts: country singer Toby Keith's 'Unleashed', which featured the controversial right-wing sentiments of the track 'Courtesy Of The Red, White And Blue – The Angry American', which applauded the subsequent US bombing of Afghanistan.

Once again, with the E Street Band back in tow, the ensuing world tour, which opened at the Continental Airlines Arena in New Jersey, was a huge sell-out success all over the world. Whatever the message of the songs on the album, there was another statement its success and that of the gargantuan tour that followed seemed anxious to make: Bruce Springsteen was back on top. A position he now seemed intent on retaining, come what may.

Certainly, the comparatively swift process that produced his next album, 'Devils & Dust', released in April 2005, seemed to back that up. There had been a year off the road once 'The Rising' world tour ended, but this time there would be no filler compilations or live releases to make up the time. Instead, Springsteen returned to Thrill Hill Studios in Los Angeles with the same producer, Brendan O'Brien, he had worked with on 'The Rising', and set about recording his most rounded, satisfyingly outward-looking set of songs since 'The River' 25 years before. The result was a 12-track opus – some of it also recorded at his home in New Jersey – that would come complete with its own intriguing the-making-of DVD documentary along with special acoustic-only versions of five of the tracks.

Not that the amplified mainstream versions of the songs were exactly evocative of the classic E Street Band sound. Indeed, the only member of the E Street Band on the new album was recent addition Soozie Tyrell on fiddle. The rest of the stark studio backing group comprised producer O'Brien on bass, Steve Jordan on drums, with further orchestrated accompaniment by the Nashville String Machine. In fact, the albums 'Devils & Dust' most resembled were 'Nebraska' and 'The Ghost Of Tom Joad'. Full of obvious country, blues and folk influences, more than a few of the songs had, in fact, originally been penned during the solo acoustic tour that had ensued in the wake of the 'Tom Joad' album a decade before. As Springsteen explained at the time, *"I wrote a lot of this music after those shows, when I'd go back to my hotel room. I still had my voice, because I hadn't sung over a rock band all night. So I'd go home and make up my stories."*

There had actually been plans to release them as a kind of companion-piece to 'Tom Joad' before the more compelling idea of an E Street Band reunion meant they got put on the creative backburner for the foreseeable future. When the 9/11 attacks then inspired the new set of songs that resulted in 'The Rising', the idea of making a third-in-the-series of acoustic-based albums was delayed still further.

As a result, some of the tracks on 'Devils & Dust' actually hark back lyrically to a pre-9/11 America that no longer existed outside the songwriter's imagination; the fear of global terror taking a back seat to the more colloquial concerns of family trust, long-held dreams, both lost and found, and the hopes and fears of the everyman, now middle-aged, that Springsteen had been singing about in one form or another, on and off, since he was a young man still finding his way, looking for simple escape.

Typical of this idea was the track 'All The Way Home', actually written some 15 years before, ostensibly for a 1991 Southside Johnny album – and the nearest the new album comes to rock'n'roll, based around the story of a girl the narrator picks up in a seedy bar to the background noise of 'some old Stones' song the band is trashin'...' Much more explicit, however, was 'Reno', a musically straightforward acoustic number but one which resulted in the album being forced to carry an 'adult content' sticker, featuring as it does the story of a visit to a prostitute, including direct references to anal and oral sex. While 'Black Cowboys', built around a melancholic piano figure, also concerned itself with the grittier side of life – several long, wordy verses and no chorus at all, detailing the rite-of-passage of the appropriately named Rainey Williams and his early days growing up in the ghetto where his only respite is watching old cowboy films on TV.

The rest of the album ranged across a similarly esoteric list of subjects: 'Silver Palomino' (an impossibly romantic Tex-Mex border ballad about a boy's love for his horse – really!); 'Jesus Was An Only Son', featuring church organ and gospel-tinged backing vocals and a suitably biblical lyric that namedrops Nazareth and Gethsemane; 'The Hitter', another solely acoustic number but one of the album's major highlights, lyrically, about a once-successful boxer now fallen on hard times; 'Long Time Comin'', a gorgeous country-flavoured ballad about a pair of lovers expecting their first child; or the enigmatic title track itself, which starts with a lone acoustic guitar before gradually building via piano and strings into a true Springsteen epic, and one of the few post 9/11 songs on the album, written from the perspective of a young US solider in Iraq, its pay-off line unbelievably poignant: *"What if what you do to survive/kills the things you love?"*

"All the songs are about people whose souls are in danger or at risk," Springsteen explained in the 30-minute DVD film that accompanied the album. *"They all have something eating at them. Some come through successfully and some come to a tragic end."* Directed by Danny Clinch and shot in New Jersey in February 2005, the film also featured full-length solo acoustic performances of the title track, 'Devils & Dust', plus 'Reno', 'Long Time Comin'', 'All I'm Thinkin' About' and 'Matamaros Banks'.

In keeping with the new album's more intimate, stripped-down feel, the live shows Springsteen performed to promote its release featured him as a solo artist again. Appearing at London's Royal Albert Hall in May that year, he delivered a blistering solo set focused chiefly on material from the new album, along with songs from both 'Nebraska' and 'The Ghost Of Tom

Bruce Springsteen Glory Days – 50 Years of Dreaming

Chapter Eight

Joad', plus acoustic versions of several numbers from 'The Rising'. Older songs were kept to a minimum, though he still found room for heartfelt old chestnuts like 'It's Hard To Be A Saint In The City' and 'You Can Look (But You Better Not Touch)'.

But the biggest surprise was yet to come, which was the announcement just before Christmas 2005, barely six months after the release of 'Devils & Dust', of yet another new Springsteen album in the offing, planned for release in May 2006, barely 12 months on from its predecessor and marking the speediest succession of albums in Springsteen's career since 'The Wild, The Innocent & The E Street Shuffle' swiftly followed 'Greetings From Asbury Park' over 30 years before.

Most surprising of all, however, was the other chief distinction of the new album: it would comprise an entire set of cover versions – and not just any cover versions but an entire 13-track album's worth of the songs, all interpretations of traditional material originally written by or associated with the legendary American folk singer Pete Seeger. Titled, 'We Shall Overcome: The Seeger Sessions', on paper it may have sounded less than appetising to the generation that first 'discovered' Bruce Springsteen through albums like 'Born In The USA' – Bruce swapping his trademark R&B-inflected sound to pay tribute to an artist who had, in his time, stood tall against what he once saw as the corrupting influence of rock'n'roll (it was Seeger who led the protests when Bob Dylan first unveiled his new electric sound at the 1965 Newport Folk Festival) – but in time it seems destined to become one of his best-loved. All doubts were swiftly dispelled, in fact, as soon as the strident banjo that introduces opening track 'Old Dan Tucker' kicked in. Indeed, the most obvious difference between the new album and both the Springsteen albums of original material that had immediately preceded it was how much this one jumped out at you.

If describing it as 'rocking' would be wide of the mark, material like the riotous 'Jesse James' and 'Jacob's Ladder' fair jumped out at you and swung you round the dance-floor like nothing else the Boss had done since his 'Born To Run' heyday. But then the Boss had never had such a luxuriantly appointed band to back him. For not even the E Street boys at their height could match the lengthy cast of musical companions Springsteen had assembled for this album – an 11-piece band (first convened for two tracks on a 1998 Pete Seeger tribute album) augmented by a full horn section and backing singers, including wife Patti on vocals and additional guitar, all belting out the tunes with just-about reigned-in abandon. Or as Gavin Martin described it in his ebullient review for Uncut, 'mixing a Cajun two-step with a Mexican percussion fiesta, it all adds up to a great teeming flood of Americana: the streams of high mountain

Bruce Springsteen *Glory Days – 50 Years of Dreaming*

Chapter Eight

Bruce Springsteen *Glory Days - 50 Years of Dreaming*

Chapter Eight

Bruce Springsteen *Glory Days - 50 Years of Dreaming*

Chapter Eight

Appalachian bluegrass, running into Afro-Caribbean swells and bluesy stomps and hollers. The legacy of another flood, the one occasioned by Hurricane Katrina, emerges time and again.

Not just in the abundant New Orleans musical references, but in the apprehension of the mighty river rolling in the prayerful 'Shenandoah', the acknowledgment that there'll be No more water/Fire next time in the defiant gospel chorus of 'Jacob's Ladder', and of course in the Civil Rights-bred resilience of the slow-burning title track.'

And of course it was uncanny how so many of these old, almost forgotten songs vibrated with modern resonance, from the anti-war slant of 'Mrs. McGrath' to the joyously uplifting – and positively surreal! – 'Froggie Went A-Courtin', and off on another completely different, this time much darker tangent with the plangent Crescent City funeral march of 'Oh Mary Don't You Weep'.

Recorded as live, not in a plush LA studio this time but in the more authentically gritty surrounds of Bruce and Patti's makeshift New Jersey ranch-studio, 'We Shall Overcome', as Seeger himself was quick to acknowledge, was more a tribute to the defiant spirit that originally powered this ancient-sounding music than it was to the man who wrote and/or resurrected so many of the songs first time around. Discussing the new album when it was released, Springsteen said, *"So much of my writing, particularly when I write acoustically, comes straight out of the folk tradition. Making this album was creatively liberating because I have a love of all those different roots sounds... they can conjure up a world with just a few notes and a few words."*

Writing in the extensive sleeve notes that accompany 'We Shall Overcome: The Seeger Sessions', Springsteen summed the album up best when he described it as *"a carnival ride"*, characterising the music as *"the sound of surprise and the pure joy of playing. Street corner music, parlour music, tavern music, wilderness music, circus music, church music, gutter music, it was all there waiting in those old songs, some more than one hundred years old. It rocked, it swung, it rolled. It was a way back and forward to the informality, the freeness and the eclecticism of my earliest music and then some."*

Once again, the world tour to promote the album has been a surprise package, Springsteen assembling an expanded 17-piece version of the same 'Seeger Sessions Band' that accompanied him on the album in what has been billed as 'an all-new evening of gospel, folk and blues'. In addition to Springsteen on vocals, guitar and harmonica, the full line-up comprised the following: Sam Bardfeld (violin), Art Baron (tuba), Frank Bruno (guitar), Jeremy Chatzky (upright bass), Larry Eagle (drums), Charles Giordano (accordion, keyboards), Curtis King (vocals), Greg Liszt (banjo), Lisa Lowell (vocals), Eddie Manion (sax), Cindy Mizelle (vocals), Mark Pender (trumpet), Marty Rifkin (pedal steel guitar), Richie 'La Bamba' Rosenberg (trombone), Patti Scialfa (vocals), Marc Anthony Thompson (vocals) and Soozie Tyrell (violin). Kicking off the tour with a series of ten highly-publicised shows in Britain and Europe – following an initial one-off US date in New Orleans on April 30th – tickets for all of which sold out literally within minutes of going on sale, the US tour resumed with a series of 18 shows commencing in Boston on May 27th and scheduled to finish in New Jersey on June 25th. Commenting on the excitement and sense of anticipation generated by the announcement of the shows, legendary UK concert promoter Harvey Goldsmith said, *"We announced Bruce Springsteen's concerts in the UK at 9.00am on Friday 7th April. By 9.10am both shows had sold out. This is the fastest-selling show ever in Manchester!"*

But then, as an unsurprised Steve Van Zandt shrugged and said, *"It's as close as people are going to come to Woody Guthrie and Pete Seeger."*

Springsteen now admitted that there was a certain element of what he called *"intimations of mortality"* about where he found himself in his life and career.

In his 1998 lyrics-and-anecdotes book, Songs, he had commented, *"When you get the music and the lyrics right, your voice disappears into the voices of those you've chosen to write about... But all the telling detail in the world doesn't matter if the song lacks an emotional centre. That's something you have to pull out of yourself from the commonality you feel with the man or woman you're writing about."*

As long as he continues to feel that way about his music – our music – one thing we can be sure of is that there will be plenty more of those stories to come.

Chapter Eight

Bruce Springsteen *Glory Days - 50 Years of Dreaming*